THE RAINBOW
CIRCLE OF EXCELLENCE

THE RAINBOW CIRCLE OF EXCELLENCE

by
Riley Wallace

with
Michael D'Andrea and Judy Daniels

WATERMARK PUBLISHING

This book is dedicated to our human family around the world,
who suffered together through the dark hours of September 11, 2001.
Now more than ever, it is important to keep our hopes
and dreams alive, to continue to strive for
personal and collective excellence over the rainbow.

A portion of the proceeds from this book
supports the University of Hawai'i
Special Fund for Athletic Enhancement.

Editors
George Engebretson
Tom Chapman

Design and Production
Gonzalez Design Company

Photo Credits
© Ralph Omoto (front cover, right inset back cover,
pp. ii, vii-viii, 23-25, 27, 56-57, 72 top, 96-97,
113-118)
© CW Pack Sports (left and center insets back cover,
pp. 72 bottom, 73-75)
© Jamie Schwaberow/WAC Photos (p. 26)
Derek Inouchi (background back cover, p. 28)

Library of Congress Control Number: 2001097152
ISBN 0-9705787-6-8

Watermark Publishing
1000 Bishop Street., Suite 501-A
Honolulu, Hawai'i 96813
Telephone: Toll-free 1-866-900-BOOK
e-mail: sales@watermarkpublishing.net
Web site: www.bookshawaii.net

Printed in the United States of America

CONTENTS

ACKNOWLEDGMENTS

Many people were instrumental in bringing *The Rainbow Circle of Excellence* to print. The authors are grateful for the valuable comments and suggestions of Tom Chapman, who reviewed the original manuscript. We would also like to extend a very special thanks to George Engebretson and Watermark Publishing. George was with us on every step of our journey to capture in words the excitement and joy of the Rainbow Warriors' championship season.

Thanks also to Coach K and Hugh Yoshida for helping introduce the book, and to Ralph Omoto, whose fine photography documented our season both on and off the court.

Given the book's emphasis on positive family spirit, we'd like to extend our most sincere thanks to our own family members.

To Joan Wallace, Rob Wallace and Kim Wallace Haynes: thank you for the support, encouragement and love you have given over the years.

To Shawn D'Andrea and Kara Pitt-D'Andrea: thank you for the joy, inspiration and ongoing hope you provide.

And a special thanks to the youngest members of our families: Jackson Riley Haynes and Mahealani D'Andrea-Daniels, just for being who you are. You'll always be the stars on our team!

PREFACE

by Hugh Yoshida
Director of Intercollegiate Athletics
University of Hawai'i

Recent years have brought an astronomical rise in the popularity of U.S. college athletics — due in part to the expansion of women's sports on college and university campuses. That, of course, warms the hearts of athletic directors everywhere. It's fan support, after all, that lets us maintain high-quality athletic programs that address the special needs of student-athletes.

As a one-time college football player, I understand what a wonderful opportunity it is for young men and women to participate in college athletics. It lets them realize their athletic potential at a level of competition that few people are able to experience, while giving them a chance to get an education and develop life skills at the same time.

Because we at the University of Hawai'i recognize the powerful impact that athletic programs have on our students' overall development, we are genuinely committed to providing the support and resources that they need to succeed — athletically, academically and personally. This book fits well with that philosophy, in its behind-the-scenes portrayal of how our men's basketball program helps players reach their personal goals.

I have long respected Riley Wallace's straightforward, matter-of-fact style — both on and off the court. Now, in *The Rainbow Circle of Excellence*, he uses these down-to-earth teaching methods to communicate his values in ways that are both instructional and inspirational. You'll learn a great deal about Riley and his coaches and players in these pages, but even more about the simple steps you can take to realize your own dreams, regardless of your career or calling.

And, in the bargain, you'll enjoy the story of a basketball team's championship season — a story I believe will be reprised many times in the years to come.

FOREWORD

by
Coach Mike Krzyzewski
Duke University

As the head coach of Duke's men's basketball team, I let my players know right from the start that "excellence" is the standard they are expected to achieve on the court. But like Riley Wallace, I believe that excellence is truly measured by the way each of us strives to realize our unique potential for greatness in our personal lives, careers and academic endeavors. I believe that an important part of a coach's responsibility is inspiring athletes to wake up every morning ready to live that day with passion, enthusiasm, respect for others, and a desire to attain the specific goals that guide their lives.

While coaches can encourage young people to strive to lead lives of excellence, it is ultimately up to each individual athlete to develop the personal visions, goal-setting skills and desire to realize his or her personal potential for greatness. Certainly, being able to establish and attain a clear set of individual goals is important in life. But from my perspective, the essence of life involves being a part of a family, team, school or organization — groups whose members have the opportunity to use their unique skills and abilities to promote a collective vision of success, and who are genuinely motivated to do so.

A well-respected member of the fraternity of college coaches, Riley Wallace has now written a book that helps clarify the tremendous role that coaches can play in promoting human excellence. His book provides much more than just a report on the success that the members of the University of Hawai'i men's basketball team attained during the 2000-01 season. It is really a story about the importance of creating — and realizing — dreams. His ideas hold relevance for all of us: teachers, parents, business and community leaders, doctors, lawyers, youth workers and what Riley refers to as "plain folks" who want to lead more effective and satisfying lives.

Coach Wallace stresses the importance of building a positive sense of community within any group. Indeed, the steps he takes to nurture a family spirit in his team can be easily applied to a wide variety of other groups and organizations. I especially value Riley's approach to building respectful connections with people from cultural and racial groups that are different from our own. This is critical given the tremendous cultural changes now underway — not just in colleges and universities but in society in general. Riley Wallace provides an optimistic view of what it takes to promote group unity, with implications that go far beyond his team's championship season. What's more, he offers specific suggestions for building such unity in our groups and organizations.

Why read Riley's book? Because you're a college basketball fan who likes Cinderella stories. Because you're curious about what a basketball coach could possibly have to say about leading a life of excellence. Or, best of all, because *The Rainbow Circle of Excellence* is full of useful ideas for realizing your own potential for personal greatness.

INTRODUCTION

There are several reasons I decided to write this book with the help of our sport counseling and development specialists, Dr. Judy Daniels and Dr. Michael D'Andrea. First, I wanted to share some of the lessons I've learned during my 15 years as a head basketball coach — lessons in leadership, excellence and building a positive sense of community. I realize that many books have already been written about these virtues. A number of them are written for people who are presently in leadership positions or who want to become recognized as leaders in a particular field.

But this book is different. It focuses on some of the ways you can achieve a higher level of excellence and develop the qualities of a good leader — whether or not you aspire to a leadership position. Whether you're striving to become a more effective manager, trying to be a better parent or just looking for ways to lead a more productive life, I believe you'll find our Rainbow Warrior experiences instructive. With this in mind, I describe my own model for effective living — the Rainbow Circle of Excellence — in Part One.

Second, I wanted to write a book that would give our wonderful fans a more personal glimpse into the University of Hawai'i men's basketball team and, in particular, the championship season of 2000-01. I see this book as a way to give our supporters a better understanding of the values that guide our coaching philosophy. I often say that we have the best fans in the country, and I truly believe that. They consistently give so much to our teams, and this book is one small way to thank each of them for their years of support and loyalty. Part II includes dramatic, inspirational stories about our coaches and players, to help our fans get to know them better. These stories show how different types of leadership abilities helped us achieve excellence and realize our collective vision of success.

Third, I wanted to introduce other individuals who support our coaches and players and help our team reach its goals. In Part III you'll meet many of these people and learn about their contributions to our success. Most of them work quietly behind the scenes, but I consider all of them to be special leaders and I want to recognize them in this book.

Fourth, I wanted to write about the one thing that really sets the University of Hawai'i men's basketball team apart — its cultural diversity. Our country's shifting demographics — and the rapid globalization of our culture — challenges all of us to be more accepting and respectful of the differences in people. It's my hope that the lessons we've learned from our players and coaches will help in the ongoing effort to meet the challenges of cultural diversity, in new, positive and life-enhancing ways.

This book wouldn't have happened without the involvement of Drs. Daniels and D'Andrea. Besides working full-time in the University's Department of Counselor Education, these professors have been sharing their expertise in sport counseling and performance enhancement strategies with my coaches and players since 1997. In Chapter Eight, "the docs" — as we respectfully call them — describe some of the leadership and team-building strategies they use to help student-athletes realize excellence in their lives. Regardless of why you're reading this book, I believe you'll find their techniques interesting and useful in your own life.

The voice in this book is mine, but the docs are responsible for helping me present my ideas clearly and concisely. I've also asked them to add some of their performance enhancement activities at the end of each chapter. These Excellence Activities are designed to make this book interactive. They are similar to those used with the players, and you might find them useful in learning about what I call "excellence over the rainbow."

I use this term throughout the book to refer to whatever your "pot of gold" might be — the one that lies at the end of your personal or professional "rainbow." For college basketball coaches and players, that might mean a winning season or a bid to a post-season tournament. For college students, it could mean a diploma on graduation day. A business person might see excellence over the rainbow as a big promotion. For parents, it might simply be quiet recognition for the role they've played in raising respectful and responsible children. Whatever it is you are striving to achieve, it's my hope that these Excellence Activities can help promote life changes for those who choose to try them.

Whether you're reading this book as a college basketball fan, as a student, or as someone seeking a motivational nudge, I hope *The Rainbow Circle of Excellence* will help you find a greater level of satisfaction in all your life's endeavors.

PART ONE

THE RAINBOW CIRCLE OF EXCELLENCE

Excellence can be attained if you…

care more than others think is wise…

risk more than others think is safe…

expect more than others think is possible…

dream more than others think is practical.

— *Author unknown*

CHAPTER ONE

OUR CHAMPIONSHIP SEASON

As the final seconds ticked off the clock, I took the time to experience the joy of the moment. I could smell the popcorn and hear the home crowd heading for the exits. And I could feel the electricity you sense in the air when something really special is happening.

It was March 10, 2001, and the University of Hawai'i Rainbow Warriors basketball team was about to celebrate something that many people had said was impossible. We were going to win the Western Athletic Conference tournament and earn an automatic bid to the NCAA national championship. We'd already beaten highly-favored Texas Christian University and Fresno State University on two of the past three days, and now we were going to win in overtime against the favored Tulsa Golden Hurricane — a team backed up by 8,000 rowdy fans in their own Reynolds Center. In short, we were going to the "Big Dance!"

As the clock ticked down and I began bringing our regular guys off the court, I was nearly overwhelmed with the emotion of the moment. I tried to connect with each of them — these players from all over the world who had taken us so far so fast. I greeted our always steady but now exhausted senior guard, Nerijus Puida. Going in for him was Lane O'Connor, another senior, who had brought a special kind of leadership to this team as a backup player.

With less than 30 seconds remaining, I high-fived the game's hero, Canadian freshman Carl English, who I replaced with the always energetic, five-foot-four Lance Takaki, a fan favorite back in Honolulu. And I watched as Mike McIntyre, one of the hardest working, most dedicated players on the team, pumped his fists in the air as he left the game for another ecstatic guard, junior Ryne Holliday.

I looked down our bench with only a couple of seconds left and saw Troy Ostler, our starting center and top rebounder, sidelined for most of the game with an ankle injury. The grin on his face was wider than the ice pack on his ankle, and it spoke volumes about the celebration we were about to share.

I looked at our gutsy top scorer, Predrag "Savo" Savovic, beaming with excitement, and next to Savo, freshman forward Phil Martin, throwing a towel into the air with a Rainbow victory yell. And there was five-foot-ten freshman guard David "Jeep" Hilton, jumping on the backs of our two tallest players — six-ten freshman center Haim Shimonovich and his seven-foot backup, Todd Fields. And then the final buzzer made it official, and the thousands of fans stood and applauded their Tulsa team and our players, too — for the tenacious way these Rainbow Warriors had overcome their long odds.

Who would have believed this? A true rainbow of players from a half-dozen countries and dramatically different backgrounds, joined together just a few months earlier to set — and reach — this ambitious group goal. Here was Savo, a young man from war-torn Montenegro, now a key reason for our team's success. And Jeep, who rose above his homeless, inner-city background to find a niche on this determined Rainbow team. And Carl English: Not long ago he was just a skinny kid shooting baskets into the night on a deserted country road in Newfoundland. Tonight he was the star player in the 2001 WAC championship game.

This shining moment at Reynolds Center was a direct result of all of the sacrifices we had made during the season, sacrifices forged by a collective vision of success. It took a lot more work, sweat and tears than anyone had imagined as we pushed for the level of excellence we knew we could achieve as a group. There's no question we'd had our ups and downs during the season, and sometimes it seemed there were lots more downs than ups.

I thought back to the previous November when, with six games under our belt, our record was a disappointing two wins and four losses. The sixth game was a low point: an embarrassing 84-64 loss at UCLA's Pauley Pavilion, when we were beaten in every aspect of the contest. But that game was also a wake-up call for our players. We knew then that a complete turnaround was in order, were we ever to achieve the excellence we hoped for.

And so the turnaround began. We proceeded to win five of our next seven games, and even finished second in the Rainbow Classic, the tournament we host at the Stan Sheriff Center, our home court on the University of Hawai'i campus in Mānoa Valley. We were beaten in the finals by a University of Tennessee team that was then ranked sixth in the nation, in a game that was much closer than the final score of 69-58 indicated. This was a particularly important run in that we played several of these games without Troy Ostler, our leading rebounder and number-two scorer. Troy had suffered a severely sprained ankle during our 100-86 win against the University of Alabama-Birmingham, in the championship game of the Nike Festival Tournament. Having to play those games without him was an early test of the team's ability to endure difficult times. By winning our next two games against scrappy University of Manhattan and equally feisty St. Louis University, our coaches and players were starting to sense that we could indeed overcome adversity. We were beginning to understand that the team had the kind of grit and resilience that individuals and groups need to achieve excellence.

In the games to follow, however, our sense of optimism would be sharply tested. We lost five of the next six. Four of them were on the road, against Texas Christian University (103-64), Southern Methodist University (69-56), Rice University (70-64) and the University of Tulsa (79-67). But then our fortunes rebounded, as the team won six of the remaining games before the WAC Tournament. One of these was an important confidence-building 91-73 win over 19th-ranked Fresno State University at home. That late-season run and the amazing success we then achieved at the WAC Tournament really defined the character of our team and cemented the commitment to excellence by both players and coaches.

The Ups and Down of Basketball

People who are familiar with the idiosyncracies of college basketball know that the sort of roller coaster season we experienced is not at all uncommon. All basketball teams experience highs and lows in the course of a season. It's part of my job as head coach to try to understand why these ups and downs occur. Over the years I've found three main factors that predictably make this happen. They certainly contributed to the Rainbow Warriors' roller coaster ride during that championship season.

First is the learning curve. At the start of the season, players learn the various offensive plays and defensive strategies that my coaching staff and I have designed for them. This is especially challenging for freshmen and junior college transfers who simply aren't accustomed to the fast pace and pressure of playing at the Division I level. What's more, when we first began practicing in October 2000, we told all the players they'd be learning a brand new offense. Having carefully assessed the strengths of each player during the off-season, I had decided on big changes in our game plan from previous years. Given the athletic talent and potential this team showed, I wanted to use an offensive strategy with considerably more ball movement. In seasons past, we'd used an offense I called "G-game." Ball control is a key consideration in making the G-game work. That means I placed a lot of responsibility on our guards. Our teams had experienced much success with the G-game. It was particularly effective in 1996-97 and 1997-98, when star guards A.C. Carter and Alika Smith led our teams to back-to-back 20-game winning seasons. The Carter-Smith tandem was probably the best one-two punch at the guard positions since I've been head coach at UH.

Now, however, the combination of less talented guards and the fact that our opponents were getting used to our G-game led me to change the offensive game plan for 2000-01. Reviewing our new and returning players, I knew we were well-equipped to develop a less predictable offensive game plan, one that would surprise many of our opponents. I called this offense our "flex game." To make the flex offense work effectively, all of our players would need to be constantly involved in the movement of the ball once we brought it up court. I felt this would work well because so many of our players possessed such good passing skills and because they were obviously motivated to learn the flex offense.

At our first practice in October 2000 I explained our new approach to ball movement. Every player would be expected to pass quickly in a pre-planned strategy, while the others would make specific moves designed to confuse their defenders. I also emphasized that with the flex offense we'd be using many more back door plays, setting more picks than we had in the past and overall, playing a more patient game. Patience is an especially important virtue in making the flex offense work. I repeatedly reminded our players throughout the season that by constantly passing the ball, making the prescribed cuts and waiting for their defenders to make a mistake, they would eventually find open shots.

I was convinced that this plan, when properly executed, would rattle our opponents. But I also knew it was going to take time for our players to learn the rudiments of this new game plan and become comfortable executing it in competition. Though the guys liked the new offense, I realized that it would be a while before they got used to it. This meant that I'd have to do something that I neither enjoy nor am particularly good at: learning to be patient myself, and realizing that we'd probably lose a couple of games early in the season as the team mastered the offense.

And that's exactly what happened early in the 2000-01 season. In the first test of the flex offense against a Division I opponent, it was clear that our players needed more time to learn to execute it effectively. The 86-71 defeat in our season opener — against a very mediocre Louisville team — told me we had a lot of work to do. Our players showed some improvement in our next game, beating Southwest Louisiana University, 59-55. They looked even better in a close 65-63 loss to the University of San Diego in late November. But then they seemed to forget everything we'd been trying to teach them in that embarrassing defeat at UCLA.

In regrouping from that one, our players spent a lot of time studying the film of the game in Pauley Pavilion, mostly observing their lack of patience on offense. Meanwhile, they continued to work hard in practice and demonstrated the sort of discipline necessary to learn a difficult new task. This hard work paid off as they showed noticeable improvement in a close home loss to Georgia State, 65-63. But then things really began to kick into gear as our team went on a four-game winning streak over California State University-Northridge (76-70), the University of Alabama-Birmingham (100-86), Manhattan University (81-67) and St. Louis University (75-67).

Toward the end of the season, our players began to consistently execute the flex offense the way I'd known they could. As a result, they were able to win several games by confusing more talented teams. "Your guys are throwing the other teams for a loop with that offense," coach Jerry Tarkanian told me after we'd beaten his Fresno State team in the WAC tournament. "We just couldn't figure out what you were going to do whenever you brought the ball down the court." Thanks to our players' execution, the element of surprise and a disciplined offense had helped beat one of the winningest coaches in college basketball history.

Another factor that all too often contributes to a roller-coaster season is an inescapable part of athletics — injuries. In 2001-01 our mid-season slump had much to do with the fact that Bosko Radovic, our freshman forward from Montenegro, broke his leg in mid-December and shortly after that, we lost Troy Ostler and Mike McIntyre for several key games with sprained ankles. Injuries were probably the main reason we dropped those six consecutive road games in January and February. Once our players were healthy and injury-free, we were able to realize our potential for greatness at season's end. We won seven of our last eight WAC games from February 15 through March 10, including wins over Southern Methodist University (79-65), Rice University (61-53), and Texas Christian University (102-87), and we posted our first road victory of the season when we beat San Jose State, 71-61. In fact, our only conference loss during the season's final month was to the University of Texas at El Paso, in what I felt was the best road game we'd played up to that point.

But despite these key injuries and the growing pains of the new offense — not to mention the 22-game suspension of Haim Shimonovich for playing on a team of professionals back in Israel — our players and coaches never got down on themselves. The staff remained confident of the team's abilities, and the players continued to trust the coaches' wisdom, working hard to master the plays that could lead us to victory. And our sport counseling and development specialists helped us focus on our individual and collective strengths.

All of this contributed a great deal to what is commonly referred to as a team's "chemistry," the combination of intangibles that includes:

- Players' willingness to buy into the strategies that the coaches dictate
- Players' willingness to sacrifice individual goals and glory in order to realize team goals
- Coaches' and players' commitment to avoid distractions and to focus on those collective goals
- The degree to which players and coaches develop a positive sense of community to meet challenges together throughout the season

To be honest, I can think of several previous UH teams I've coached that were able to learn new plays and strategies faster than the 2000-01 squad. But what really distinguished this championship team was the unique group chemistry that the players, coaching staff, sport psychologists and other support personnel created over the course of the season.

After we won the WAC and accepted our trophy, we were off to Dayton, Ohio, for the opening round of the NCAA Tournament. We had drawn as our opponent the tough Orangemen of Syracuse University. We lost that game, 92-78, and it wasn't pretty. For all our hard-earned chemistry, what's interesting is how the distractions of success disrupted that chemistry in Dayton. Most of these distractions came from players' parents, other family members and, especially, girlfriends who flew in from around the U.S. and Canada to cheer us on against Syracuse.

Though many of our fans weren't aware of it at the time, another major distraction involved one of our team's most important players. After we'd won the WAC tournament someone had apparently suggested that Savo Savovic was violating NCAA rules. He had, they claimed, played for a professional team while he lived in Yugoslavia. And so, as we prepared for the Syracuse game in Dayton, we were also caught up in a flurry of meetings and conference calls involving NCAA officials, our lawyers and Savo himself. We argued the allegations against Savo and tried to determine if he would be allowed to compete against Syracuse. As it turned out, he was finally given clearance to play by NCAA officials — believe it or not, at 5:30 p.m. on game day.

I'm convinced that the time, energy and emotional turmoil that Savo experienced during this ordeal contributed to his flat performance against Syracuse. Beyond its adverse impact on Savo, this unwelcome controversy undermined the positive and focused chemistry that our team had worked so hard to develop during the season.

What else could go wrong? Well, one of our most consistent and stabilizing players — Nerijus Puida — came down with food poisoning the night before the big game. Although Nerijus was treated by our medical staff during the night and received intravenous treatment to replace seriously depleted bodily nutrients, he had to ask to be taken out of the game at halftime. "Coach," he said to me in the locker room, "I am hurting this team, not helping them. You need to take me out," I knew then that something was very wrong with him. Nerijus is one of those special athletes who will play through pain to help his team. But neither would he bring his team down if he couldn't make a positive contribution. His illness was another variable that detracted from our team chemistry.

After Syracuse ended our magical season that night, I spent a good deal of time in deep reflection. I kept going back to the special chemistry and positive family spirit that this team had created, how the players and coaches fought through adversity to overcome the odds and achieve a level of excellence that few people expected. I also thought about what I'd do differently. Here's one thing: at Dayton we'd relaxed some of our usual policies about pre-game activities, as we let the players celebrate their victories in Tulsa. But the next time we're scheduled to play as big a game as the one in Dayton, I definitely won't let them be distracted as they were by family and friends. We'll stick to our game plan, both on and off the court.

As I reflected on the season, it also dawned on me that most people don't know a whole lot about the University of Hawai'i men's basketball family, except what they read in the sports pages. Most fans know our won-lost record and perhaps a bit about the players. But the 2000-2001 season was really more than just a sports story, and that Rainbow Warrior team was a special one in many different ways. Most important, it was a team that found its own way to achieve what we in the UH basketball program call "excellence over the rainbow."

Excellence Over the Rainbow

The rainbow is the traditional symbol of University of Hawai'i athletic teams. It represents a collective commitment to strive for excellence in all competition. It's also a constant reminder of the great rewards — the pot of gold, to stretch the analogy — that awaits those who work hard enough and smart enough to make their vision reality.

By overcoming all odds, the 2000-01 men's basketball team certainly found its own pot of gold at rainbow's end. But the concept of "excellence over the rainbow" has a much broader meaning in these pages. When I use the phase here, I'm asking you to consider your own goals and potential rewards.

Throughout this book, I will encourage you to think about the hopes and dreams you have for your life. Essentially, these dreams represent your personal rainbows. If you keep a picture of these "rainbows" in your mind, you'll be better able to overcome the difficult challenges that sometimes darken the sky.

Certainly, different people have different visions of their personal rainbows. For an athlete, a rainbow might mean winning an event for which he or she has spent thousands of hours preparing. For a teacher it might mean the act of inspiring students and helping them develop new ways of thinking. People in business might see their rainbows as generating a greater profit margin or closing an important deal. And parents might view their rainbow as the way that time, energy and sacrifice can guide their children to responsible adulthood.

Obviously, there can be as many different "rainbows" as there are individuals. Yet, I'm convinced that achieving success requires each of us to do certain things in our day-to-day living.

- Find something in life to be passionate about
- Effectively communicate your passion
- Learn to endure life's frustrations and disappointments
- Bounce back strong and enthusiastic from adversity
- Accept responsibility for your actions
- Demonstrate discipline as you set out to accomplish your goals
- Create a positive sense of community with your friends and colleagues

In the spring of 2001, our team headed for the WAC Tournament with a barely respectable record of 14 wins and 13 losses. Few observers in the conference gave the University of Hawai'i Rainbow Warrior basketball team much of a chance to win the tournament. We were the decided underdogs, even if we were already on a roll. We'd won four of our last five regular season games, but the teams we were scheduled to play in the tournament were comprised of individuals with more overall athletic ability than our players. None of our team members had been as heavily recruited as other players in the WAC and around the country. Some people thought our players were lucky just to have the opportunity to play at the Division I level of college basketball. Our guys were considered to be just average athletes in the highly competitive world of college sports.

On the other hand, I knew that as a special kind of community, no other team could hold a candle to us. I did see the Rainbow Warriors as a true "community," driven by an intense sense of unity and a strong desire to succeed. When a group of common people come together with this sort of collective heart and spirit, the chances of achieving unexpected success increases exponentially.

Lessons for "Plain Folks"

One of the most important things I've learned during my 15 years as a head coach — and especially as a result of working with the 2000-01 team — is that ordinary people can accomplish extraordinary things by making a real commitment to excellence. Fundamentally, this requires us to do two things. First, it asks us to exert the time and energy to develop the skills, knowledge and attitudes that are necessary to deal with the stormy times of life. Second, it demands that we move beyond our perceived differences to build a positive sense of community — a strong family spirit within the group of which we are a part.

As a head basketball coach I've worked hard over the years to master these two goals. Though I haven't always succeeded, I now see clearly how a commitment to these ideals can lead to a more effective and satisfying life. Beyond the willingness to build a sense of community, we also need to keep in mind that achieving excellence requires a lot of hard work.

Since I was born and raised in a working class family from rural Illinois, the notion of hard work seems natural to me. While I might have gained some measure of celebrity — or sometimes notoriety — in sports circles, I still identify strongly with my working-class roots, and I genuinely enjoy being accepted as "just plain folks."

I think this is one of the reasons why I hope other plain folks will find our Rainbow Circle of Excellence interesting and useful. Much of the credit for any success I've found along the way must go to the everyday people who've taught me that life is more than awards, titles or special promotions in a career.

I once heard a tree used as a metaphor for succeeding in life. This idea made a great deal of sense and has stuck with me ever since. The saying goes like this: "Greatness in life does not depend on the bark that you wear, but the fruit that you bear." To me, one of the most important legacies we can leave lies in helping other people realize their own unique potential for excellence and effective living.

This is why we in the basketball program work so hard to nurture not only our players' athletic abilities, but their personal and academic potential as well. The metaphor of the tree reminds me that greatness in life can be measured by two yardsticks:

- How well we realize our own potential for excellence
- The way we help others lead effective and satisfying lives

My hope is that the success of our basketball program will be judged not only by won-lost records and tournament victories, but also for the way we've taught our players to realize excellence in their personal lives. This is the fruit I genuinely hope to bear in life.

Learning From My Mentors

Much of what I've learned about coaching has come from the people that I've played for, worked with or coached against over the years. I owe a great deal of gratitude to six individuals in particular who served as important mentors for me, and who greatly influenced my thinking about life in general and coaching in particular. My first true mentor was Dale Daughtery, my basketball coach in junior high school. Coach Daughtery was the one who ignited my interest in the game when I was a youngster in Jerseyville, Illinois. His competitive nature had been nurtured by his experiences in the United States Marine Corps. Besides helping me learn the basics of basketball, he greatly reinforced the work ethic that I was taught at home.

My second mentor was Coach George Havens, who led our Jerseyville High School basketball team. Not only was Coach Havens a great coach, he was a terrific teacher of life. It was from him that I learned what a powerful role coaches can play to help players develop the attitude and personal skills they need to lead effective, satisfying lives.

Next, I was fortunate to play basketball for Coach Orvis Sigler at Centenary College. Prior to accepting the head coaching position at Centenary, Coach Sigler coached at West Point, where he was well-respected for the disciplined and passionate way he worked with his players. Besides teaching me a great deal about the game of basketball, he taught me about character, a sense of responsibility and respect for others. Coach Sigler was much more than a coach to me. After my father was killed in an automobile accident during my sophomore year, he took me under his wing and provided the kind of support and guidance I needed to get through that difficult time. He was truly an important father figure whom I admired very much. It was Coach Sigler who helped me gain the confidence and knowledge about the game that would enable me to become a head coach myself. And it was Coach Sigler who gave me my first college coaching job, when he hired me as his assistant when I graduated from Centenary in 1964.

After my first season as an assistant coach, Coach Sigler's wife passed away. He decided then to retire from head coaching and become the school's athletic director. To fill his big shoes, Centenary hired as its head coach Joe Swank, who had been coaching at Tulsa University for the previous 19 years. Coach Swank was a strict disciplinarian and one of the best basketball tacticians I have ever had the pleasure to work with. As his assistant for three years, I developed a great deal of technical knowledge about the game. I also acquired the kinds of organizational skills that any head coach needs to be successful in this business.

The fifth person who I consider an important career mentor is Larry Little, my predecessor at the University of Hawaiʻi. Larry and I lived in nearby towns when we were youngsters. We played against each other in high school and later worked together at Litchfield High School in Illinois, where he was head coach and I was his assistant. Later in his career Larry replaced Coach Swank at Centenary. Among his other accomplishments there, he helped center Robert Parish develop into the well-rounded All-American who would go on to star with the Boston Celtics. As Coach Little's assistant for 13 years, I learned that great coaches do not always get the credit they deserve. And make no mistake about it, Larry Little was a great college basketball coach. More than a mentor, Coach Little became a lifelong friend who taught me much about life, hard work and staying committed to my dream of being a head coach myself.

Stan Sheriff, the former athletic director at the University of Hawaiʻi, was the person who finally made that happen. In the summer of 1987 Stan invited me to Hawaiʻi to talk about accepting the UH head coaching position. Hawaiʻi hadn't had a winning season in four years and was pretty much a cellar dweller in the WAC. But in my conversations with Stan, I believe he saw me as the kind of person who could turn the basketball program around and make it a winner. Stan knew how to build a new head coach's self-confidence, and he taught me a great deal about what it takes to be successful. Stan Sheriff was one of the most important mentors, professional advisers and friends that I've ever had.

Learning From My Colleagues

I've also learned a lot from the coaches our teams have played against. They have showed me many things I wanted to emulate and many things I definitely wanted to avoid. Three of them deserve mention here.

In college basketball the name Bobby Knight is synonymous with high standards, winning and excellence. Few head coaches in the history of the college game have enjoyed as much success as Coach Knight. He may be controversial, but he is also one of the finest basketball coaches ever. His record speaks for itself. No other coach can boast NCAA and NIT championships as well as Olympic and Pan American gold medals among his many achievements. Only two coaches in college basketball history have won more than the three national championships that Bobby won with Indiana University. His coaching achievements have been honored in many ways, including induction into the National Basketball Hall of Fame in May 1991.

Only Coach Knight and University of North Carolina head coach Dean Smith have both coached and played on NCAA Championship teams. Bobby helped Ohio State win it in 1960, while Dean did the same for the University of Kansas in 1952. Coach Knight has also been recognized as being one of the youngest head coaches to win 200, 300, 400, 500, 600, and 700 career games as a college coach. He is one of only 13 coaches in college basketball history to record 700 or more victories.

I had the pleasure of coaching against Bob Knight just once, when the Rainbows opened the 1997-98 season with an 82-65 upset win over his Hoosiers in Stan Sheriff Center. I have a tremendous amount of respect for the man, based not only on his record, but on the high standards of excellence that he sets for his student-athletes. While many college coaches with enviable won-lost records have dismal player graduation rates, Bob Knight demands excellence both on the court and in the classroom. If I have learned anything from watching him over the years, it is the importance of setting high standards for both the "student" and the "athlete" sides of the student-athlete. While his fiery disposition and behavior eventually led to his dismissal from Indiana, I know he'll find continued success in his head coaching position at Texas Tech University. Regardless of what his critics may say about Bob Knight, I am certain that his leadership style and standards for excellence will ultimately boost Texas Tech to a consistent national ranking.

Within our own conference, the WAC, I've learned a lot about the psychology of college coaching from Billy Tubbs at Texas Christian and Jerry Tarkanian at Fresno State. It's been suggested in the media that my relationship with Billy Tubbs is a negative and contentious one. That really isn't true. I respect Coach Tubbs and the winning tradition he has brought to every program he has worked with. He is a much better coach than he gets credit for and very good at getting his players to perform beyond even their own expectations. I also appreciated the fact that, after we won the WAC Championship, Billy was the first person to call and congratulate me and wish us well in the NCAA tournament.

From a psychological perspective, I have learned several good lessons from Billy Tubbs. One of them is the way he can work referees to his advantage during a game. Let me give you an example. A few years ago, Billy brought his high-scoring Horned Frogs into Stan Sheriff Center. We were doing fine matching their players both offensively and defensively, and we took an early lead in the first half. All of a sudden Billy went on one of his famous theatrical outrages, this one directed at one of the refs for making what he thought was a bad call against TCU. Billy's heated comments unglued the ref, who then called a technical foul against him.

But even after calling that foul, the ref continued to engage in a discussion with Billy, holding up the game. I walked down the sidelines to find out why. Our team had the momentum at that point in the game; now we had a chance to build a substantial lead, and I didn't want to lose it to Coach Tubbs' slowdown tactics. But the ref was so upset by Billy's comments that when I asked him about the delay, he turned on me and gave me a technical foul too!

Needless to say, I was very upset at being on the receiving end of the ref's misdirected anger. I began yelling at him when, out of the corner of my eye, I caught a glimpse of Billy grinning broadly. Finally it dawned on me what he'd done. Billy had purposely worked up that official into such a state that he knew the ref would overreact if I got into the act. And that's just what happened. Sure enough, the time it took for the players to take their technical foul shots was just enough time to slow the momentum we had enjoyed. Billy had used the delay tactic masterfully. It was the kind of mind game that successful coaches like Billy Tubbs use to gain the upper hand in competition.

When you think about excellence in college coaching, it's difficult not to think about Fresno State's Jerry Tarkanian. To call this man a college basketball legend is an understatement. Tark is one of the most gifted pied pipers that the college game has ever seen: he has consistently accepted players with troubled pasts who are looking for opportunities to redeem themselves. While the risks he has taken with some of these young men have had less-than-happy endings, I genuinely respect Jerry for giving them a chance when other coaches closed their doors to them. I also respect Tark for his ability to consistently achieve national rankings and for the record crowds he draws wherever he coaches.

Like Bob Knight, Jerry has been involved in his share of controversy. Nevertheless, I believe that his sheer coaching ability — as well as his commitment to giving troubled kids a chance — far outweighs any criticisms directed against him. Playing against a Tarkanian-coached team is like being in a high-stakes chess game. He makes so many strategic moves that it's a challenge just figuring out exactly what he's trying to do. He is so good at coaching that he makes me want to beat his teams just a little bit more than other teams we face during the year. So in preparing to play Fresno State, I always work extra hard with the coaching staff to come up with something that will throw "the master" off base. You can imagine how we felt when our players worked our flex offense so effectively against his Fresno State team in the 2001 WAC tournament.

I felt especially good about that upset because of the big games Jerry has won against us in the past. His teams beat us twice in very close games during the 1996-97 season, forcing us to share the WAC title with Fresno State that year. And then there was the emotionally-draining 85-83 loss to his Bulldogs in the semifinal game of the National Invitational Tournament — on our own home court at the end of the 1998-99 season. So while I felt good about our upset of Fresno State in the 2001 WAC tournament, I also knew it wouldn't last forever. Tark has such a strong desire to beat you every time he plays you, that I was soon thinking about the games we'd play against them during the 2001-02 season.

During the off-season, I bumped into one of his assistant coaches during a trip to the mainland. "Riley," he said with a sly smile, "we're concerned about that new offense you threw at us in Tulsa. We've been spending a lot of time watching the game film."

"I'll bet you have," I thought. "I'll bet you've studied film of the flex and already come up with ideas on to how to beat it." I knew I'd better start thinking of a new ways to catch Tark off guard next time — new ways to outfox the fox. It's a chess game, and it never ends. And I have to admit I find it personally challenging and lots of fun as well.

While all of my mentors and fellow coaches emphasize the importance of hard work and discipline, they've all had different ways of thinking about the game and coaching their players. I've learned that to be a successful head coach is to take the time to try to understand these diverse views and approaches. In a broader sense, I've learned that understanding the different ways that other people think and react is an important life skill, one that can be extremely useful in the pursuit of excellence.

Excellence and Cultural Diversity

The word excellence can be used in many ways. When I use it here, I'm referring to much more than winning a WAC championship and an NCAA tournament bid. Beyond this athletic achievement, I had the opportunity to witness how excellence can be achieved when people from different backgrounds and countries come together, work hard to build a special family spirit, and learn important lessons about life from one another in the process.

I am convinced that the way our team performed on and off the court was in large part a reflection of what they had learned from these important life lessons. Although they may have been judged as "ordinary" college athletes by some in the business, I viewed the players as very special indeed — not only for their ability to overcome enormous odds on the basketball court, but by the way they tackled dramatically difficult personal challenges to achieve athletic excellence.

Often during the season I would look down our bench and marvel at the special attributes of our individual athletes. Sometimes I would see Predrag

Savovic, a young man who'd spent part of his childhood in war-ravaged Yugoslavia. Though Savo had experienced the kind of stress that most American youths can only imagine, he had somehow found a way to maintain a positive enthusiasm for life that was contagious.

Or I'd find myself looking at Haim Shimonovich, our freshman center from Israel, another country that is endlessly buffeted by inter-ethnic conflict and violence. What had it been like for him, a member of the Israeli army, to deal with the constant threat of random violence? Haim told the team psychologists that the new challenges of being a student-athlete at the University of Hawai'i were nothing compared to some of the stresses of his recent past. From my perspective, Haim's positive attitude and ability to respond to such challenges represented the kind of personal strength that would benefit any team he played on.

Like the others on the team, Savo's and Haim's cultural backgrounds played a major role in the way they've developed as individuals. Not surprisingly, they became fast friends and constant companions when the team went on the road. Once as we flew to the mainland for a game, I noticed that Haim was sitting next to Savo. On closer inspection I discovered that the Israeli, with paper and pen in hand, was trying to teach the Montegrean how to speak Hebrew. Although I've been told that Hebrew is one of the most difficult languages to learn, it was obvious to me how enthusiastically Savo accepted the challenge. At the same time, Haim seemed very proud to be able to share this part of his culture with a teammate. This was just one example of how the cultural differences that characterized our team worked to draw us closer together.

Our international players also attracted considerable interest and support off campus. Through Nerijus Puida, for instance, I learned about Hawai'i's Lithuanian community, whose members often called him to invite him to various weekend activities. I'd lived in the Islands for more than 20 years and never dreamed that such a Lithuanian community existed.

Sometimes the touches of home were unexpected, as when Savo ran into a group of sailors from Montenegro. The sailors were on an extended stay in Hawai'i while their ship was being repaired and during that time, they came to several of our games to cheer on their countryman. Savo was delighted.

Haim Shimonovich became involved with Hawai'i's active Jewish community when a member of Honolulu's synagogue called to say he was welcome to celebrate the Sabbath with them on any Friday he was available to attend. This sort of hospitality is very important for any student-athlete, but especially one whose home is more than 8,000 miles from Hawai'i. Haim showed his appreciation to the man who called by inviting him and his family to our home games.

Even before my UH experience, I was no stranger to racial diversity issues in institutional athletics. When I was an assistant coach at Centenary in the early 1970s, I recruited the first African-American player ever to play basketball there. He was Claudell Lofton, a young man from Louisiana. Claudell was a hard-working student-athlete who played well during his four years at Centenary and graduated with a degree in business. Despite the nagging fear of having a cross burned on my front lawn — an all-too-common occurrence in the South at the time — I never regretted recruiting him. Claudell was one of the most honest, personable and upstanding individuals I have ever had the chance to coach.

But until the 2000-01 season, most of my previous experience in diversity was limited to the dynamics of white, African-American and homegrown student-athletes from Hawai'i. I had never had the opportunity to work with a team in which the majority of players came from so many different cultures and nations as the 2000-01 Rainbow Warriors. In fact, I initially had some real concerns about possible conflicts and tensions I believed might occur over the long season. That's all the more reason why I was so amazed at the way our coaches and players came together to achieve the excellence we did, despite our cultural differences. Ironically, those dramatic cultural differences actually helped us develop a level of unity that I believe few college team ever achieve. I really didn't expect to learn as much as I did about the positive potential of cultural differences. But the knowledge that I gained was yet another example to me of how we can all learn and benefit from the unexpected.

Learning from the Unexpected

Long ago I learned that to be effective a head coach must always have a game plan with specific strategies to follow as he prepares for each game. I've also learned that, while you can have the most logical possible plan prior to a basketball game, you'd better be able to deal with the unexpected situations that inevitably occur and use them to promote positive outcomes.

The huge popularity of college basketball in the U.S. is partly due to fans' anticipation that a highly favored team can always be upset by a less talented one. Who can ever forget the victory of Coach Jim Valvano's North Carolina State team over the highly-favored University of Houston in the 1983 NCAA championship game? Or the stunning December 1982 upset of number-one-ranked University of Virginia by Honolulu's unheralded, little-known Chaminade University? Or, even closer to home, the incredible 76-65 defeat of the number-two Kansas Jayhawks by the unranked University of Hawai'i Rainbows in December 1997?

College coaches will readily tell you that upsets commonly occur when the favored team fails to maintain its focus and discipline while the underdog exerts more passion and enthusiasm in striving to win the game, even if it is less talented athletically. This was certainly the case when we lost a home game to Georgia State during the 2000-01 season. I really believe we had the better team, and I know our coaching staff had worked hard to develop a game plan that could lead us to victory. In the final outcome, none of that mattered. Although we led by a point with seven seconds left in the game, a couple of our players failed to keep up their defensive intensity. Georgia State went from one end of the court to the other and scored with a put-back of a missed shot. That winning basket at the buzzer left our players — and the home crowd — stunned, frustrated and, of course, greatly disappointed.

From the perspective of excellence, it is important to recognize that while such unexpected happenings are indeed disheartening, they always represent an opportunity to learn and develop. Because I believe there's nobody who hates to lose a game as much as I do, it's rather difficult for me to find much positive about a loss like that one. But as the season progressed, I often thought about how the unexpected ending of the Georgia State game really drove home an important truth for our players. It's a lesson that's as much about life as it was about basketball: When you lose focus and intensity in an important task, you aren't likely to achieve the success or level of excellence you're after. On the positive side, I also noticed that the players responsible for letting Georgia State score at the buzzer didn't make that mistake again the rest of the season!

Focusing on the Positive

When I sense that something unexpected is happening in a game, especially if it jeopardizes our chances to win, I quickly evaluate the strengths and weaknesses our players have demonstrated up to that moment. Then I call time to talk to the team and help them refocus on our game plan. What I try to do during the timeout is encourage them to recall the positive things we did earlier in the game. I remind them to use those strengths to avoid the kind of mistakes that could cost us a victory.

From time to time we find ourselves with unexpected challenges at work, at school or in our families. I'm convinced that dealing with and learning from the unpredictable is key to achieving excellence in life. Many of the books I've read about excellence and leadership do not emphasize enough the importance of learning new and positive things from unforeseen situations. Some of these books provide "road maps" that lead people to believe that a prescribed series of steps can be taken to achieve excellence in life. On the contrary, I don't believe it is necessary to follow a step-by-step set of strategies to discover your innate leadership abilities and success potential. More important is the ability to develop a positive attitude in the face of the unexpected — helping you build on your personal strengths and improve on your weaknesses.

That said, I don't mean to downplay a game plan that provides guidelines for success. In fact, such personal plans are essential in learning how to lead a more effective and satisfying life. But I have also come to appreciate the role that the unexpected can play in personal development. I now see that these occurrences are unique learning opportunities that can propel our personal growth and development in ways that otherwise might not be possible. Rather than being frustrated, fearful or resentful of these situations that occur in your life, it is useful to recognize how they can help you find and develop untapped strengths.

Building On Strengths to Move Beyond Weaknesses

There's a tendency in our society to accentuate the weaknesses of an individual, team, or organization rather than to focus on the strengths. This kind of thinking only helps perpetuate what I call a "deficit perspective." People who operate from a deficit perspective tend to overlook their unique strengths and, in doing so, unconsciously undermine their ability to achieve excellence in their lives. More specifically, they fail to think about the ways in which they've already used their personal strengths to deal with stressful or unexpected events. Bottom line: it's important to understand and consciously affirm your personal strengths in order to move beyond your weaknesses.

When you operate from a deficit perspective, the positive energy required to learn new ways of leading successful lives is dissipated. Over the years I've noticed that college athletes seem to benefit in several ways if they can maintain balance in thinking about excellence. Our players are more energized when we help them offset the negative by reminding them of their unique basketball strengths.

Focusing on strengths motivates people to move beyond their personal limitations. A case in point: the two big men on the 2000-01 team. As we prepared for the season, I knew that Troy Ostler, our starting center, had the potential to be a dominant force in the Western Athletic Conference. To realize this potential, however, Troy would have to overcome his tendency to be soft on defense. Privately I would talk to him about his offensive strengths and shot-blocking ability, while I also spent a lot of time demonstrating the defensive intensity that was necessary for him to become a more complete player. By making him aware of his unique strengths, I tried to encourage his confidence. Troy not only appeared to feel better about himself, he typically returned to practice motivated to work on the specific weaknesses that were holding him back from realizing a higher level of athletic excellence.

Todd Fields, meanwhile, will always be remembered as an easy-going seven-footer who worked hard despite his athletic limitations. He was clearly hampered by a history of knee problems that limited his mobility and speed. As a result of his past injuries, he didn't have the offensive or shot-blocking capabilities of a Troy Ostler. Nevertheless, Todd was one of the most respected and well-liked players on our team. He was respected for his work ethic, his commitment to play despite his knee problems, and the unselfish way he worked in practice to help the other players improve — especially Troy.

To help Todd recognize the important role he played on the team, I made it a point to give him positive feedback by focusing on his strengths. I would comment on his ability to maintain a positive attitude, his endurance in playing through pain, and his willingness to play hard against Troy in our practices. It was only natural that Todd wasn't happy with his limited playing time. Yet it was also apparent that the positive feedback he received helped him mature as a person and achieve a greater level of excellence as a key backup player. As the season developed I watched him use his increasingly more positive attitude to motivate other players, especially those who were down on themselves because of mistakes they'd made in games. He also talked to his teammates about the importance of enduring long, hard practices, often bringing humor into the discussion, and he became one of Troy's staunchest supporters and friends. Although Todd didn't receive the kind of attention that other players got from our fans and the media during the season, he consistently helped others strive for excellence, in their playing and in their lives in general.

Striving for Self-Improvement

As a head coach, I always look for opportunities during practices or games to compliment my players on their athletic strengths. I do this so that they will continue to work to correct their weaknesses. Periodically, I will take them aside and ask them to tell me what they think are their own strengths and weaknesses. My experience with Lane O'Connor provides a good example of how this strategy for excellence can work.

Lane was an exceptional high school and junior college player. He had starred for Columbia River High in Vancouver, Washington, averaging 18 points per game. What really caught our attention, however, was his performance at Santa Rosa Junior College, where he averaged 19 points and 5.5 rebounds per game during the 1998-99 season. We were even more impressed with the fact that Lane had led all other junior college players in the country in three-pointers that season — hitting an amazing 51 percent. For his numerous accomplishments at Santa Rosa, he had been named to the All-Bay Valley Conference first team in 1999.

Like many junior college athletes who transfer to a major four-year university, Lane found the transition to Division I basketball more challenging than he expected. Because I had some concerns about his ability to outplay his opponents, he didn't get as much playing time as I knew he wanted during his first two seasons as a Rainbow Warrior. Despite his disappointment, he was one of the hardest workers on the 2000-01 team. But for all his excellent work ethic, I could tell that Lane's level of self-confidence had been affected by his lack of playing time. For example, he began hesitating to take open shots, both in games and during our practice sessions.

After one particularly rigorous practice before the start of the 2000-01 season, I pulled a very tired Lane aside. I told him he was one of the best shooters on the team and reminded him that this was the reason we had recruited him. I also told him that it seemed I had more confidence in him than he had in himself. To help him make a stronger contribution to the team, I said, he needed to shoot more often in practice and during games.

Of course, I knew that Lane wouldn't shoot more just because I told him to. He needed to regain some of the confidence he seemed to have lost during the previous season when his playing time had been limited. To motivate him, I not only had to boost his confidence in himself, but I had to ensure that the other coaches and players realized how much confidence I had in Lane's shooting abilities.

How did I communicate this message? During our practices I would periodically shout to the players, "Give Lane the ball. He's our best shooter. He needs to have the ball more to shoot it!" As a result Lane was persuaded to use his shooting strengths and along the way, he also regained his confidence. Like Todd Fields, Lane didn't enjoy nearly as much playing time as he would have liked. But I greatly respect the aggressive offensive game he displayed when he was on the floor, by taking and making most of his shots during practice. What I admire even more about this young man is the way he grew as a person during the two seasons he played for us. I watched him develop a better understanding of his strengths and weaknesses and demonstrate a commitment to change that made him a more effective Division I college basketball player. Among his obvious strengths:

- He worked very hard on our scout team to challenge the starting players to prepare for each game.
- He showed strength of character by remaining resilient, even when his playing time was limited.
- He fostered a positive team spirit with a unique style of humor in his interactions with other players and our coaches.

Team players like Lane O'Connor and Todd Fields constantly remind me of the things we all need to do to lead effective lives and achieve excellence. The insights I've gained from my players led me to create a model for effective living that I call the Rainbow Circle of Excellence. But before we take a tour around that circle in the next chapter, I invite you to try the following Excellence Activity, in hopes that it might help you gain a better understanding of your own personal strengths.

EXCELLENCE ACTIVITY

Goal Setting

Dr. Judy Daniels, one of our team's sport counseling and development specialists, has developed a Self-Improvement Plan for our players. This plan helps them identify specific goals that they are willing to work toward during the school year. It's a performance enhancement tool designed to help players set clear goals and achieve excellence in their personal, academic and athletic lives.

Dr. Daniels' method is a straightforward one. She asks them to complete three sections of the Self-Improvement Plan, each focusing on the personal, academic and athletic challenges that they face. Specifically, the players are asked to:

- List two or three of their personal, academic and athletic strengths
- Specify a weakness they'd like to work on in each of their personal, academic and athletic lives
- List two short-term and two long-term goals in each area
- Briefly describe specific strategies they will use to realize these personal, academic and athletic goals

Having seen the success that many of our players have experienced with this Self-Improvement Plan, I'm now a firm believer in this approach — and in the way it can help people realize their potential for excellence in different aspects of their lives. The fact is, anyone can modify Dr. Daniels' plan to fit his or her personal needs. For example, you may be interested in realizing a greater level of excellence in your career, or in your parenting skills, or in your physical health and conditioning. Whatever area of your life you may want to work on, I think you'll find the following exercise helpful.

1. Take some time to think of at least two personal, academic (or career) and athletic (or just physical) strengths you possess.

2. Focus on a particular personal, academic-career, or athletic-physical weakness you'd like to improve. Be as specific as you can in identifying this weakness.

3. Come up with at least one short-term and one long-term goal you will commit to achieving in a given time frame. Your short-term goal should be directly related to your long-term goal. For instance, if one of your long-term career goals is to get a promotion, a good short-term goal might be working toward the Employee of the Month award in the next quarter. Again, avoid being vague; it's important to be specific about what you want to accomplish.

4. Think of at least three specific things you are willing to do consistently to achieve your short- and long-term goals.

5. Take action! Remember to be consistent in taking steps to reach the goals you've set.

6. Take time to periodically evaluate your progress. Make any necessary modifications in your Self-Improvement Plan. I believe that this plan, conscientiously applied, will help you realize a greater level of excellence in your life. ●

At Stan Sheriff Center, Troy Ostler goes up for two against Tulsa (*top*)
while on the sidelines, the coaching never stops.

Our early-season game at UCLA's Pauley Pavilion started on a high note (*opposite, top*)
but ended with long faces on the bench (*bottom, left to right*: Troy Ostler, Ricky Terrell,
Jeep Hilton, Mindaugas Burneika, Nerijus Puida, Todd Fields, Lane O'Connor and Lance Takaki).
Above: Savo gets some quick pointers on his way back into the game.

On March 10, 2001, we surprised everyone except ourselves, winning the WAC championship with a 78-71 upset of Tulsa on the Golden Hurricanes' home court. *Top:* The guys on the bench count down the final seconds. *Above:* The champs pose for pictures.

Our magical season ended a week later at the NCAA Tournament in Dayton,
with a 92-78 loss to the Orangemen of Syracuse. We came up short despite the guys' gritty
play (*top*) and the support of all the great Hawai'i fans who traveled to Ohio.

A version of the Rainbow Circle of Excellence hangs in our locker room at Stan Sheriff Center, a constant reminder of the way all of its components work together.

CHAPTER TWO

THE RAINBOW CIRCLE OF EXCELLENCE

My experiences — both on and off the court — have prompted me to develop a set of values that outline what it takes to achieve excellence in life. This philosophy is summarized in what I call the Rainbow Circle of Excellence, a teaching and coaching tool that we use with our players (opposite page). The original hangs in our locker room — a constant reminder of its principles before and after practices, during halftimes and after every home game we play.

The circle is the perfect symbol of what it takes to live a more effective life — and not just because a basketball is shaped that way! The road to effective living is a lifelong journey. There's no "right" starting or ending point. Rather, it's an ongoing process in which people recycle their challenges, frustrations, setbacks and personal successes at different points in their lives.

That means that the road to effective living is not, as some suggest, a series of steps in which you must move from Step A to Step B to Step C and so on, until you've finally mastered the skills and knowledge necessary to achieve excellence. Rather I have learned that this journey involves many unexpected bounces along the way. These bounces include both opportunities and setbacks that we all experience in our careers and personal lives.

What exactly is the Rainbow Circle of Excellence? It's an interlocking series of useful skills and traits shared by successful people who lead effective lives. Let's examine these skills and traits one by one.

Interdependent Leadership: No One Can Do It Alone

I consider myself a very fortunate person. I've been blessed with a career that has taught me much about what it takes to lead an effective life and achieve excellence in the process. The Rainbow Circle of Excellence represents the culmination of what I've learned from my fellow coaches and players, a result of all the challenges and triumphs we've faced together over the years.

The first component of this model focuses on leadership issues in general and on what I call "interdependent leadership" in particular.

This is a different way of thinking about the concept of leadership because it emphasizes that we're all responsible for decision making in whatever group we're part of. None of us is an island unto ourselves, to paraphrase John Donne. Consequently, none of us is able to develop by ourselves the skills, knowledge and attitudes that are necessary to lead an effective life. In essence, good leaders learn to build strong, positive and interdependent connections with others in their group.

Certainly, my years as a head coach have taught me a great deal about interdependent leadership. But my family has also been a tremendous source of inspiration in this area. While many people think of me as a very independent leader and coach, the fact is I owe much of my success in college basketball to my wife, Joan, and my two children, Kim and Rob. They have provided endless support and encouragement and helped teach me the importance of working together as a family unit.

Only rarely have I encountered anyone able to regularly put into practice all of the characteristics in the Rainbow Circle of Excellence. While I do believe that it's important to work hard at developing these characteristics, it's simply not realistic to think we can routinely incorporate these traits in every endeavor of our lives. One of the wonderful things about being part of a well-functioning family, team, group or organization is that we are able to rely on the support of other people to help pull us through difficult and challenging times.

Rainbow basketball fans will recall how this played out in that final game of the 2001 WAC Tournament, when Troy Ostler fell and hit the floor hard midway through the first half. As he clutched his ankle in pain, you could really feel for him; it was the same ankle he had injured earlier in the season. By the expression on his face I could tell we'd be finishing the game without our star center.

More adversity struck only a couple minutes later, not long after our team trainer, Jason Goo, had helped Troy into the locker room. Now the referee whistled a needless foul on Savo. When I say "needless," I mean that the player Savo was defending had gotten a quick step on him and was heading to the basket. As the Tulsa player drove the court with a full head of steam, Savo lurched forward and bumped him. As the referee called the foul Savo also grimaced — not in pain, but in frustration at having committed an obvious foul.

At this moment I knew I had to take Savo out of the game. It was his third personal foul and the game wasn't even half over. As he walked to the sidelines, he threw a towel in disgust, muttering angrily to himself in his native Montenegrean. Now our other players would have to step forward to replace

Troy and Savo, the two guys we'd come to depend on most in difficult games.

But while another team might have folded in such a critical situation, I remained confident we could still win, even with the loss of those two key players. My confidence was rooted in an awareness that this group of young men had really connected as a team toward the end of our season. They had demonstrated the sort of discipline, enthusiasm, resilience and commitment it took to overcome unexpected adversity. Despite the many contributions that Troy and Savo had made during the season, we had not become overly dependent on their skills. Each player on the team realized he might be called on to play a productive role during the game, to help realize the collective vision we shared as a team.

In this sense we were a truly interdependent and connected group of individuals, willing to work hard to achieve a high level of excellence. Without that, we wouldn't have been able to maintain our focus or to sustain the energy required to upset Tulsa. We used our collective will power, hope and inspiration as weapons to overcome an adverse situation and in the end, victory was ours.

By that point in our season we had learned to develop the sense of interdependence and connectedness necessary to succeed. But just as important was the fact that the players and coaches created a common vision of success during the season, then worked together to make that shared vision a reality.

Creating a Vision: The Essence of Excellence

Creating a positive vision, or "visioning" as some call it, involves the act of seeing with your mind's eye. Every college basketball coach I know has this ability. They can formulate an image of how they want the season to progress. They create a mental picture of the events required to win specific games and fashion a winning season. Coaches constantly exercise this visioning ability during practices and games, developing images of different plays they want their players to use as the situation demands.

During our practices and games I constantly create images about the ways I want our players to perform. As I consider Mike McIntyre's strengths as a player, for instance, I can see him in a specific play designed to free him up to make a three-point shot at a critical point in a game — just as he did during the championship final against Tulsa.

In my mind's eye I envision how Savo's enthusiasm for the game can rejuvenate other players who may be tiring in the closing minutes of a contest — just as he did at the end of the second-round game of the WAC tournament against favored Fresno State.

Near the end of our season I frequently played a mental tape of Haim Shimonovich, our six-foot-ten freshman center from Rishon LeZion, Israel, using his size and defensive ability to disrupt other teams' game plans — and then saw how useful these strengths could be in the WAC tournament against offensive-minded Texas Christian University.

By visualizing these images before they happen, I'm better able to make quick decisions in the heat of competition. My visions, by the way, are self-adjusting. They are altered by the feedback I get from other people whom I respect. In this regard, I am lucky to work with a group of coaches who help me reshape my vision for our team as they discuss their own views of what we can achieve. Associate coach Bob Nash and assistant coaches Jackson Wheeler and Scott Rigot are always glad to share their own unique visions with me. I am grateful for their willingness to talk in staff meetings about how they envision our team reaching higher levels of excellence. Although I accept the responsibility for implementing a specific game plan, I feel fortunate to work with a thoughtful group of coaches who are passionate and effective leaders, each in his own unique way.

Passion: Using it to Motivate Others

It's one thing to create a positive vision of excellence and another to get people to become part of that vision. You hear people in athletics, business, education and politics talk about getting people to buy into a new plan or strategy or vision. But what exactly does that mean?

To me it means more than just convincing employees or team members or voters to say yes to your vision. It involves motivating individuals to work together with a sense of collective passion to realize that vision, even if it means making personal sacrifices in the process. If you could be in our locker room before a game or at halftime, you'd certainly hear me use passion to motivate our guys to play up to their potential.

While many successful leaders are able to present a glowing vision of the future, not all of them can motivate individuals to lead more effective lives by emphasizing excellence. My view of leadership includes the ability to create an interdependent community of people who are motivated to work passionately to achieve that group's goals.

The people around me know that I'm a very passionate person. I'm intense in the way I lead my life in general and particularly in the way I coach my basketball team. Over the years, in fact, more than a few people have suggested that I should better control the way I express my passion for the game.

Among them are many of the referees in our league, who have whistled me with technical fouls for being a little too passionate during games.

I agree, of course, that the expression of passion should not interfere with a leader's ability to make sound decisions. Nor do I think that passion should take precedence over showing respect for others — including members of an opposing team. However, I have learned that one of the important characteristics of effective leadership is the ability to honestly express one's passion in ways that ultimately motivate members of a team or organization.

Expressing passion as part of a vision requires the courage of one's convictions. The passionate person must be able to express those convictions without worrying about criticism. In short, good leaders create a positive vision of the future and then share that vision with others.

As I consider the state of affairs in many families, businesses and, of course, within the world of athletics, I note a tremendous leadership vacuum. What I see are many people whose leadership potential is undermined by their unwillingness to express the courage of their convictions. I also see people in leadership positions who are unwilling to listen and learn from the ideas and visions of others. So locked into their own vision of how things should be, they often fall short of effective leadership.

The way I see it, an effective leader must be:
- Strong enough to articulate his or her vision for the group
- Humble enough to learn from the ideas and visions of others
- Passionate enough to stimulate enthusiasm and positive energy among all members of the team or organization, in order to realize the full potential of the group

Enthusiasm and Effective Communications Skills

Our basketball program certainly doesn't have the reputation of the college powerhouses — Duke, North Carolina, UCLA and the others. But I would also point out that the University of Hawai'i basketball program gained a great deal of respect around the country during the 1990s. Many factors contributed to this new respect. For starters, there's the time and energy our coaching staff has invested in the recruitment of student-athletes, in particular those who've shown the desire to realize new heights of excellence in their lives. The task of recruiting these players to our program is complicated by our location on an island in the middle of the Pacific Ocean. While Hawai'i is clearly a beautiful place to live and get an education, it is also 2,500 miles from the continental United States and halfway around the world from some of our players' home countries — Israel, Yugoslavia, Lithuania. It's a distance that many parents would rather avoid in their efforts to support their sons' education.

Besides hampering our recruitment efforts, the distance factor also affects the players and coaches during the regular season. Traveling long distances in short periods of time clearly upsets both athletic rhythm and academic focus. Yet these are facts of life that we face all the time.

One thing I've learned about leadership in such complex but unavoidable situations is that it's not particularly useful to complain about things you cannot change. Rather, it's much more productive to learn from the situation, then use the knowledge gained to communicate a vision of excellence to your team, group or organization. In other words, make lemonade out of lemons.

Being an enthusiastic and effective communicator is one of the best ways to help a team or any other group realize its potential for excellence. In his book, *Positive Coaching*, Jim Thompson writes about the important role this factor plays in creating the energy and collective understanding that team members need to succeed. Thompson points out that "positive human energy can be created and generated by the emotional enthusiasm that coaches share with their teams and by coaches' ability to clearly communicate the ideas and strategies that underlie their vision of excellence."

In that WAC tournament final, for example, this kind of enthusiasm and effective communication was demonstrated not just by our coaches but also by every player on our team. It was a big reason for our success in that championship game against Tulsa. I can still recall the intensity on Carl English's face as he passionately hollered instructions from his point guard position. I remember how Mindaugas Burneika, a first-year junior college transfer student from Lithuania, shared his enthusiasm every time he came to the sidelines during timeouts — despite playing the final minutes of the game with a bloody mouth. All our guys, starters and reserves alike, were encouraging, positive and extremely vocal: "Check him, Mike!" "You can do it, guys!" "Let's keep playing our game!" "Good hustle, Mindaugas!" "Keep it up, Phil!" "We can win this one!" "Great shooting, Carl!"

Successful coaches understand how this type of encouragement and enthusiasm can energize a team that might otherwise get down on itself. This is especially important when key players are injured, get in foul trouble or can't otherwise participate in the game. It is also important to note that while positive energy can be highly motivating, it must be balanced with the goals of the group. As the head coach, I know my job is to balance my enthusiasm with my responsibility to clearly communicate the specific strategies we need to implement. For that reason, I made it a point during timeouts at Tulsa to look calmly into the eyes of each player and tell him, "We're going to win this game if you stay focused and listen to what I want you to do next." Not only did each player listen and stay focused, they effectively followed each direction I gave them. As a result, when the tournament was over, we had changed our image from a group of ordinary athletes to champions who could play well against anybody.

Over the years I have come to understand the vital role that effective communication can play in the creation of a successful life. You can have a wonderful vision for a group, and the group members can have endless passion and enthusiasm, but unless they are able to communicate with others they are unlikely to be successful.

Fortunately, I work with both coaches and support staff who have developed strong interpersonal communications skills. These people have found a variety of effective ways to communicate their ideas, passion and enthusiasm to others. Their different styles of communication give me some wonderful alternatives when I must ask a staff member to talk with:

- A player who is homesick or depressed about his lack of playing time
- Parents who are undecided about whether they want their son to play basketball in far-off Hawai'i
- The media when they're looking for a new angle on our team
- A professor concerned about a player's academic performance

Effective communication is included on the Rainbow Circle of Excellence because I know that this life skill is vital in achieving excellence in all walks of life. This is true whether you are a business person negotiating an important deal, a doctor discussing a medical concern with a patient, a mechanic explaining a car problem to its owner, a teacher helping a student or a parent fostering a child's unique gifts.

Being an effective communicator is a primary key to success. Communicating well with others enables us to successfully negotiate our day-to-day challenges, as well as the more long-term difficulties we face in our lives.

Endurance and Resilience

Success does not come easily. Usually, the achievement of excellence in life requires us to be resilient and endure unexpected difficulties. Given the important role that endurance and resilience play in the Rainbow Circle of Excellence, it may be useful to reconsider the definitions of these terms. According to the American Heritage Dictionary, endurance is "the act or power of withstanding hardship, such as stress or strain; persevering." Similarly, resilience is defined as "a person's ability to recover from disruption and misfortune."

The Rainbow Warriors basketball team had to endure a number of unexpected hardships during the 2000-01 season. For starters, there was a good deal of uncertainty about the eligibility of Haim, our newly recruited freshman center from Israel. Student-athletes from foreign countries often possess unique cultural strengths and personal abilities that have a positive impact on our basketball program. Over the years I've noted that most of the foreign players we've recruited demonstrate unusually high levels of endurance — to overcome language and cultural barriers and to achieve excellence both in basketball and in the classroom. Nerijus Puida, the starting guard and co-captain of that 2000-01 team, is a good example. When he arrived on campus in 1999, this young Lithuanian had difficulty just speaking English. Two years later he graduated from UH with a 3.65 grade point average out of a possible 4.0. Not only was he one of our most popular players, he received the highest honor a student-athlete can receive at the University: The Jack Bonham Award for athletic and academic excellence. The formula that Nerijus used to accomplish these achievements was simple: Endurance + Resilience = Excellence.

Shortly after we heard from the NCAA that Haim was ineligible to play the first 22 games of the season, the team experienced another significant loss. Bosko Radovic was a freshman recruited from Montenegro, Yugoslavia, to play either the shooting guard or small forward position. But during a practice drill in December 2000, Bosko broke his leg in a freak accident that didn't even involve contact with another player. Then, for several key games during the season, we lost Troy Ostler, our center and leading rebounder; Mike McIntyre, an excellent three-point shooting guard; forward Phil Martin; and point guard Jeep Hilton. All of these players were lost to injuries.

These unexpected events definitely tested the will of our players. The younger and less experienced ones were especially affected. I'm convinced that these disruptions influenced our performance in mid-season, when we lost several games we might otherwise have won. During these trying times, however, I noticed that we still stayed together as a group. The players and coaches demonstrated the resilience that is necessary to work through such hardships.

Another reason why the team overcame adversity during these unexpected disruptions is that many of our players and coaches had successfully endured major crises at different times in their own lives. These stories of endurance are both dramatic and inspiring; you'll find them told in detail in the following chapters. They are stories that helped me create the Rainbow Circle of Excellence.

Responsibility

Most college basketball coaches talk a lot about the importance of having their players act responsibly on and off the court. I agree that accepting responsibility for one's actions is a key attribute in leading an effective life and achieving excellence. It is very difficult for any group to reach a high level of excellence unless each individual in that group accepts responsibility for his or her own actions. An all-too-easy way to fragment a team — or a business or a classroom or a family — is for one member to criticize others when things aren't going well, without taking responsibility for the way his or her own actions may be contributing to the problem.

Responsibility and trust go hand in hand. When you're part of a team of responsible people, you find that needless blame and finger-pointing are avoidable even in the worst of times. A responsible person can acknowledge when his actions are helping or hindering the group. In concrete terms, being a responsible team member means that you:

- Show up on time for practice and give 100 percent at practice and in games
- Use feedback from coaches and other players to improve your performance
- Work hard to develop new knowledge and skills that will enable you to more effectively respond in future situations

Response-ability

Rainbow basketball fans may not realize that I received a master's degree in guidance counseling from the University of Illinois. I have a genuine interest in counseling and psychology and find that the knowledge I derive from these fields is useful in my coaching work. Judy and Michael, our sport counseling and development specialists, always keep me updated on interesting new developments in these areas. One of the concepts they shared with me comes from the work of William Glasser, who calls his theory of practical counseling "reality therapy." The primary purpose of reality therapy is to help people learn more effective and satisfying ways of mastering situations in which they've previously been unsuccessful.

One of Dr. Glasser's ideas is now an integral part of the Rainbow Circle of Excellence — what he calls response-ability. What he means is that individuals must constantly strive to learn new ways of dealing with challenges if they expect to realize high levels of excellence in their lives. They can do this by expanding their response-ability — their ability to effectively react to new and unexpected challenges in their lives.

Head coaches are great candidates to become reality therapists. We are constantly pushing our players to develop new skills and abilities that enable them to respond to a broad range of unexpected situations during a game. One of the players on the 2000-01 men's basketball team who has been repeatedly challenged to learn new response-abilities is Mike McIntyre. Mike grew up in Long Beach, California, and starred at Long Beach Poly High School before coming to the University of Hawai'i as a freshman in 1998.

Mike's youthful experiences helped him develop his response-ability. When he was 11 years old, his mother often relied on him to take care of his younger brother while she worked. So Mike learned the importance of being responsible for others at an early age. And by watching how hard his mother worked, he developed his own strong work ethic that has helped him achieve excellence in other aspects of his life. Thus, Mike brings a highly disciplined manner to the way he approaches life's unexpected demands. This strong discipline and his sense of pride in a job well done are as clear in the way he plays basketball as the way he did chores around the house.

Mike started the 2000-01 season as our valued sixth man. When we needed a point guard, Mike was called on to fill that role. When we needed him to play off-guard, he accepted this challenge and worked hard to meet the different demands of that difficult position.

Committed to excellence in basketball, Mike comes to practice early and leaves late. It is not uncommon to see him shooting a hundred shots and working on his ball-handling skills long after a tiring practice. As Mike matured over his three years as a Rainbow, such discipline paid off by helping him become one of the most versatile and valued players on our team. Not only did his commitment to excellence enable him to become one of our best defensive players, his offensive response-ability paid off for him in the UH men's basketball record book: he now holds the number-eight spot in career three-point goals made.

All of us are called upon at some time in life to respond to unusual and unexpected types of challenges. To meet these challenges and achieve excellence, it is important that we strive to expand our response-ability and exercise discipline in our daily lives.

Discipline

I'm from the old school of coaching. This means I highly value a disciplined approach to my work and the way my players execute our game plan. I strongly believe our success in 2000-01 was due in large part to the level of discipline our players demonstrated on and off the court, and the way they successfully executed the plan I created for them.

Discipline is necessary to be successful in any endeavor. I believe this is true no matter what your choice of profession. If you don't consistently take a disciplined approach in whatever you do, you are unlikely to be very successful. Certainly, you will not realize the level of excellence that distinguishes outstanding entrepreneurs, teachers, taxi drivers, lawyers, surgeons, carpenters, plumbers or parents.

What do I mean by discipline? I like the American Heritage Dictionary definition, which defines it as "training that molds or perfects a specific skill or behavior. . .control that results from such training. . .to train by instruction and control." Participating in sports at any level — from elementary school kickball to college athletics — provides us unique opportunities to have fun while learning to control our thoughts and actions at the same time. In this way, organized sports teach us how to develop new levels of self-discipline. We are challenged to operate within certain parameters by learning, among other things, to follow a set of pre-established rules, not to stray out-of-bounds, and to be selfless team players.

Early on, youngsters typically require older role models like parents, teachers and coaches to provide discipline. But the ultimate goal in life is to develop an inner voice that tells you what you should be doing and when you should be doing it, without being reminded by someone else. Psychologists refer to this as shifting from an external locus of control to an internal locus of control. I call it being able to control yourself, while demonstrating the personal discipline you need to live an effective and satisfying life.

Pat Summitt, head coach of the University of Tennessee women's basketball team, talks about the important role of discipline in the pursuit of excellence in her book, *Reach for the Summit*. The level of excellence in Pat's life is apparent in her record at Tennessee: 689 wins against just 190 losses — a 78-percent winning record — and six national championships. Pat does a fine job of summarizing the tenets of discipline and explains why it's necessary to accomplish the goals you set out to realize. "Discipline is the internal mechanism that self-motivates you," she writes. "It gets you out of bed in the morning. It gets you to work on time, and it tells you when you need to work late. It drives you. It is essential to success, whether individually or in a group."

The members of the 2000-01 Rainbow basketball team achieved their high level of success because they were disciplined both as individuals and as a group. For example, the members of our scout team consistently demonstrated the kind of passion, enthusiasm and discipline necessary to realize the collective vision of success that we shared. These are the guys who see limited playing time in actual game situations but are expected to test the starting team's abilities in our practices.

Associate head coach Bob Nash works closely with the scout team. He helps them learn our opponents' offensive and defensive plays and then encourages them to "take it to the starting team" in practice. Our scout team in 2000-01 included Lance Takaki, Lane O'Connor, Todd Fields, Ryne Holliday and Ricky Terrell. These guys don't get a lot of glory; they see little game action and not much is written about them in the newspapers. Rarely will you see or hear one of them interviewed on television or radio. But despite this limited attention, our scout team players were disciplined enough to give their all at practice every day, committed enough to learn hundreds of our opponents' plays and willing to play hard enough to get our starters ready to face the challenges of every upcoming game.

All in all, these guys gave new meaning to what it means to play basketball with a disciplined, unselfish and passionate spirit. The way they accepted the challenge of playing less than glamorous roles on our team was a very important factor in the overall excellence we achieved during the WAC tournament. I watched how their commitment to hard work challenged our other players to develop untapped athletic potential. In this way, they helped our team evolve into a special kind of community that fostered excellence among all of its participants.

Creating A Family Spirit: The Community Within

The word community means different things to different people. To some it may refer to residents of a certain neighborhood or geographical area, say, rural versus urban. To others it might mean a group of people related by their unique cultural, ethnic or racial background, such as the Asian-American, African-American or Italian-American communities. Still others might use the term to describe the interdependence people have as members of the broader global community.

I think of a community as a group of people sharing common interests, goals and needs. In this sense, all of us are a part of several communities — members of a team, family, company, ethnic-cultural group or professional organization, such as a community of teachers or doctors.

The final component on the Rainbow Circle of Excellence relates to the importance of building a positive sense of community and family spirit. People use a variety of words and phrases to describe this trait. Coaches frequently talk about the importance of having a strong team spirit and how this spirit motivates athletes to make the extra effort in competition. Teachers and principals know that creating a positive school spirit inspires students to achieve a level of excellence that they might not reach in a school without this community feeling. Business leaders know that fostering a genuine sense of company loyalty inspires workers to realize their collective potential for productivity and profit. Whatever you choose to call it, I know that promoting a sense of interdependence — fostering a climate in which individuals feel positively connected with each other — helps those individuals achieve excellence in their lives.

When I was still new to the men's basketball program, I learned a powerful lesson about the importance of being made to feel valued and connected. The late Stan Sheriff — then the UH athletic director and later also my good friend — recruited me to become the head basketball coach in the late 1980s. In my first year we won only four games and lost 25. The next year, however, we were the "NCAA turn-around team" when we won 17 games and lost 13. As we entered the Rainbow Classic in December 1988, we had a 6-3 record and were facing nationally-ranked powerhouse Purdue University. We pulled off a major upset that night, beating them 72-69, and as time expired in the game, Stan rushed over and gave me one of the biggest bear hugs I've ever had.

"I had faith in you," he shouted over the buzz of the crowd. "I knew you were meant to lead this team. You're the guy we need to turn this program around. I'm so glad you're here."

It was just the vote of confidence that a new coach needed. From the start, Stan always made a genuine effort to make me part of the Rainbow sports family.

Building a positive family spirit in groups is never easy. The task is even more daunting when people from different cultural and racial backgrounds are brought together to seek common goals. You need only to look across our nation and around the world to see what I mean. Cultural and racial differences not only seem to create barriers for people working in groups, they often lead to much of the violence that occurs in the world. When you have an opportunity to be part of a culturally-diverse group that develops a strong family spirit, it is truly a special experience.

This is one of the things that impressed me so much about the 2000-01 Rainbow Warrior basketball team. This group of young men from a wide range of backgrounds was expected to share a common vision for success. They were asked to work together in a passionate and unselfish manner to achieve their collective goals. Instead of letting their cultural differences create barriers that would prevent them from realizing those goals, they used their diversity as one of their greatest sources of strength.

The members of the University of Hawai'i men's basketball team had all the ingredients to achieve athletic excellence. They demonstrated passion and enthusiasm for the game as well as the endurance, resilience, discipline and response-ability essential to realize greatness. Their most vital characteristic, however, was their ability to build a family spirit fueled by the common vision we all shared. For all of us, such a visioning process is essential in living effective lives and realizing the goals we set for ourselves.

Here's another Excellence Activity, one designed to stimulate your ability to create positive visions of your future. If you decide to try it, I hope you find it enjoyable, and that it might even encourage you to create a vision that can help you live a more effective, more satisfying life.

EXCELLENCE ACTIVITY

Vizualization

Often, the way we do things flows from the way we see ourselves. Research shows that if we don't think we're capable of performing a certain task in the way we'd like, or if we have doubts about accomplishing a particular goal, then that's what's likely to happen! However, when we can see ourselves successfully performing a task in our mind, there is a greater likelihood that our actual performance of that task will improve.

Sport counselors and psychologists use such "common-sensical" ideas in visualization training with athletes. I have been very impressed with the way our sport counseling and development specialists have helped our players increase their potential for athletic excellence by teaching them how to visualize improved performance. I've also learned that anyone can benefit by taking time to visualize how they might successfully achieve any goal. For instance, I've started using visualization when I play golf and I've found that it's helped improve my game.

Beyond athletics, people can use visualization skills to increase their performance in business, teaching or parenting. Basically this involves taking the time to use your imagination to see yourself accomplishing a specific task. You might be trying to interact more positively with a co-worker, teach a great class or complete an activity with your child. Whatever the task, using visualization can increase your self-awareness, your skill acquisition, your self-confidence and your emotional control — dealing more effectively with stress, anger, frustration, anxiety and moodiness.

To get the most out of visualizing success for yourself, it's important to keep several things in mind:

- Focus on the goal you want to achieve or the skill you'd like to improve
- Imagine yourself realizing that goal or doing the best job you can in your specific activity
- Very important: keep positive images of yourself in your mind as you visualize

Use all of your senses when visualizing. This means not only trying to "see" events unfold but to "hear" what is being said and "feel" what is going on around you. Try to pick up on any smells, tastes and emotions that come into your mind as you continue your visualization. Remember: the more vivid the image the better!

For visualization to work you have to commit to it. Like any new skill you try to develop, the more often you use it the more likely you are to experience positive changes in your targeted, real-life goal. ●

CHAPTER THREE

LESSONS IN CULTURAL DIVERSITY

I grew up in rural Illinois. I was the third youngest in a family that included three brothers and three sisters. We lived in the small river town of Grafton until I was in the fifth grade, when we moved to Jerseyville. To say that our surroundings were modest would be an understatement. I suppose you might describe our family as being "economically challenged." But while we may have been poor, my siblings and I didn't really think much about it; we were too busy helping my parents make life as good as it could be. Money was scarce, but our folks taught us not to do anything to make others look down on us.

Nowadays, it's hard for people to relate to what my life was like back then. When I talk about our outhouse, for instance, and mention a "two-holer," some folks look blank, or uncomfortable. A two-holer, of course, is an outhouse luxurious enough to accommodate two people at once!

In addition to tending a well-kept garden, my parents planted fruit trees all around our house, in the interest of maintaining a healthy diet year-round. I vividly remember the many times that my brothers and sisters picked fruit from these trees and laid it in shallow pits that we'd dug and insulated with clean hay. After that, we covered the pits with wood and dirt. Storing fruit in this simple but effective way let our family enjoy the tasty treats for months to come.

Every Saturday, my mother gave each of us a bath in the kitchen. She heated the water on the stove then poured it into the makeshift tub on the kitchen floor. From Sunday through Friday, we just washed quickly with washcloths. So it was a real treat when we moved from Grafton to Jerseyville: our new house had an indoor bathroom complete with a gleaming bathtub!

My father was a proud, hard-working man who held jobs in a dynamite plant and a glass factory. My mother worked as a housekeeper and cook for the local public school. I am particularly proud of her because at the age of 60, she finally realized her dream of graduating from college. This will give you some sense of her level of determination. I am thankful to her for teaching me the importance of enduring difficult challenges as she persevered in fulfilling her lifelong dream of a college education. My father wasn't as fortunate, however.

He was killed by a drunk driver in an auto accident when I was a sophomore at Centenary College.

Most of the people I grew up with in Illinois and even at Centenary came from the same basic background. The absence of much cultural diversity, however, was anything but a handicap. I developed values and a way of looking at the world that were directly tied to my rural, working-class roots. One of the most useful values I acquired was the strength to face life's challenges without fear, with dignity and integrity. In our little corner of the world, we were proud of being "rugged individualists."

Beyond the Rugged Individualist

Today I still value the traditional notion of the rugged individualist. I believe that individuals must be rugged to be successful in college sports, and, to a certain degree, in life. Most of the coaches who taught me used the image of the rugged individualist as a primary strategy to motivate players and, in fact, as an important part of their philosophies of life.

While rugged individualism is still important, however, the world around me has changed considerably since those early days in the Midwest. It's a long way from the factories of rural Illinois to the floor of Stan Sheriff Center. In recent years, my coaching career and my experiences as a husband and father have taught me to move beyond the notion of the rugged individualist. Now I better appreciate the benefits that come from nurturing interdependent and cooperative relationships with others. I've learned that in the 21st Century, effective leadership will involve much more than simply encouraging people to "tough it out" during difficult periods.

In our complicated times, leadership also requires a sensitive approach. It is more important than ever to communicate a genuine sense of understanding about the stresses and concerns experienced by players on your basketball squad or people on your team at at the office. Professional counselors refer to this important leadership ability as "empathetic understanding."

Empathetic understanding doesn't mean sentimental pity. Rather, it means that you understand what someone is going through in a deeply human and respectful way. It doesn't mean giving someone a handout. Rather, it builds a connection that encourages people to help themselves, to do better in their lives and, by doing so, to help their entire group succeed. We all experience rainstorms in our lives. We all know that it's good to have someone around when things get gloomy — and even better when that person helps us learn new and effective ways of dealing with stormy weather. Good leaders know that human connections marked by empathy, understanding and support inspire something deep down in people's souls.

One of the great challenges faced by the 2000-01 players and coaches was how to develop the empathetic understanding that would help the team achieve its collective vision of success. This was particularly challenging given the players' multicultural backgrounds. While the Rainbow Warriors are the current leaders in this kind of athletic diversity, it is a growing fraternity. With the demographic changes taking place around the country, college coaches will be increasingly pressed to deal with the challenge of cultural diversity in the years ahead.

The National College Athletics Association recognizes the importance of promoting "unity through diversity" in culturally and racially-diverse teams. This national organization also acknowledges that teams and academic institutions are being challenged now more than ever to create a special sense of unity in such groups. According to an article on the NCAA's Web site, "One of the challenges of a diverse group is finding a way to help the group appreciate the different contributions of its members while also unifying them to work toward a common goal. It's an issue that manifests itself on athletic teams and in academic departments across the nation every year."

The UH men's basketball program has faced these challenges and flourished. The 2000-2001 team, for example, thrived on the different strengths and abilities that the players had to offer one another. By sharing their unique life stories and perspectives with the rest of the team, both players and coaches were able to learn many new lessons. Consider Lance Takaki, the fan favorite born and raised in Honolulu, the team's only native-born Hawai'i resident. We call Lance our "local ambassador," since he's the one who helps acclimate many of our foreign players. I remember when he and Nerijus Puida were eating lunch together shortly after the Lithuanian arrived in Honolulu for the first time. When Nerijus picked up an unfamiliar set of chopsticks, it was Lance who gave him his first lesson in dining without silverware.

Lance also took the time to tell our out-of-state players about pidgin, the local dialect that's a mix of English, Hawaiian and idiomatic sugar plantation slang. Explaining pidgin wasn't always easy for Lance — trying to tell teammates, for instance, that the catch-all phrase "da kine" can mean just about anything. At the end of the season, Lance advanced his cause by purchasing copies of a little book entitled *How to Speak Pidgin*. This he shared with his pidgin "students" so they could better fit into the local scene.

What Made Them So Special?

Throughout the 2000-01 season I commented often about the "special-ness" of this team; why it was so different from other teams I'd coached. Naturally, cultural diversity came up time and time again. When we arrived in Dayton, Ohio, to play Syracuse University in the NCAA Regionals, I learned that a national journalist had described the Rainbow Warriors as the most culturally-diverse college basketball team in the country. Writing for *CBS Sports Line*, sports reporter Mark Alesia observed:

"There should be a statue off the Hawaiian Islands, but instead of Lady Liberty holding a torch, it should be a referee holding a basketball. Yes, give the University of Hawai'i your huddled masses, yearning to shoot a 'three.'

"The Rainbows, who face Syracuse on Friday in the first round of the NCAA Tournament, are a team unlike any other in college basketball. Seven players are from foreign countries. In this melting pot of hoops, there are players from several European countries, African-Americans, plus white guys from Texas and Utah. There is also one player from Hawai'i.

"'One of the things I do in a class I teach with many of these players is to ask them to introduce themselves and talk about how their home environment and family background influenced who they have become in life,' said Dr. Judy Daniels, a sports psychologist who works with the team and teaches a life skills course. 'I specifically ask each player to talk about something the other people in the class don't know about them and to briefly say something about two people in their lives who shaped them into who they have become.'

"The team's best player, guard Predrag Savovic, talks about praying for the safety of his parents two years ago as NATO bombs dropped on Yugoslavia. Freshman guard David Hilton from New York City talks about having been homeless.

"'It's unbelievable how they get our players to open up, talk about their unique cultural backgrounds, and relate to each other in positive ways,' coach Riley Wallace said of Daniels and her husband, a sports psychologist who also works with the team. 'It has drawn the players closer together which has had a very positive impact on the entire team.'"

When I read that story, I realized that to many people we probably did look like a little United Nations. Half of our players were from foreign countries — Haim from Israel, Nerijus and Mindaugus from Lithuania, Savo and Bosko from Montenegro, Phil and Carl from Canada. Players from the U.S. mainland came from cities, small towns and suburbs (Todd from Texas, Lane from Washington, Troy from Utah, Ryne from rural Illinois) and included three

African-Americans — Jeep, Ricky and Mike — from New York, Los Angeles and Long Beach, California. And then there was Lance, our homegrown product from Honolulu.

At any home game, it was easy to see how our fans and booster club members embraced and supported our cultural diversity. Members of the Kam family, for instance, brought large flags of the players' home countries to the games. Each time someone scored, one of the Kams would raise that player's flag high in the air. The gesture was just one of the ways that Hawai'i's people expressed what we call the aloha spirit.

Living in Hawai'i has taught me a great deal about the peaceful coexistence of people from different cultural and racial backgrounds. But the 2000-01 University of Hawai'i men's basketball team was easily the most diverse group I have ever had the pleasure to work with. Not many other basketball coaches have had to build cohesiveness and family spirit with so many different elements. And so I want to share some of the benefits that can be derived from working in culturally-diverse groups, plus some of the things we did to foster a family spirit on our team.

Effective Living in a Culturally Diverse Society

Future demographic indicators predict that the cultural diversification of our society will be one of our most significant challenges in the coming years. Results of the 2000 Census clearly highlight how quickly this is affecting all segments of our nation. The dramatic increase in the number of African-Americans, Asian-Americans, Latinos and Native Americans living in this country — partly because of the continuing influx of immigrants — is dramatically changing our cultural landscape. Many sociologists predict that by 2050 most of the people living in the U.S. will come from non-white, non-English-speaking, non-European backgrounds.

Consider the implications. Our country is undergoing a profound and unprecedented change. We are moving from a society once made up mostly of white European descendants to one that will be truly multicultural and multiracial, and all in a few short decades. Given the existing level of tension that still exists among different ethnic, cultural and racial groups in the U.S. and around the world, people will be increasingly challenged to get along with those who are "different" from themselves.

Certainly, you will hear more about the importance of promoting "unity through diversity" and the need for us all to become more "culturally competent" in years to come. Regardless of our field of work, we'll all need to become

Our players come to UH from near and far.
Top: Lance Takaki (*hand on ball*) with his
Honolulu youth basketball team. *Above:* A young
Mindaugas Burneika at Lithuania's Palanga
Beach in 1981. *Left:* Predrag Savovich with his
mother, Olivera, at Boka Bay in Montenegro.

more comfortable with cultural disparity. And we'll be challenged to develop new skills that will help us develop interdependent and respectful relationships.

Differences can cause conflicts. As a basketball coach I've seen how cultural or racial misunderstandings can prevent teams from developing the kind of family spirit that leads to winning seasons. Over the years, most of my challenges have involved helping white and black players develop the cohesiveness necessary for successful group interaction. Given the interracial conflicts and tensions that have historically existed in the U.S., this is no simple task.

Coping with black-white tensions will continue to have a high priority in our country. Yet future coaches, teachers, business leaders, politicians and parents will also be pressed to deal with the impact of global multiculturalism. This means that people will have to gain a better understanding of many "between-group differences." For example, I knew that Lance Takaki's sense of humility and quiet demeanor was due in no small part to his Asian-American background and values. And I understood that the way many people in Western European countries are raised is reflected in the assertive and confident manner that Savo presents himself on and off the court.

While I've gained some understanding of how these between-group differences define the way players act on a team, I've also learned not to over-generalize. There are "within-group differences" that exist in every cultural and racial group in the world. In fact, I have been told there are more differences among people who come from the same cultural group than there are among those who come from different ones.

One of the major challenges we face in the years ahead is to not only learn to tolerate our differences, but to see how they can lead us to become more respectful of human diversity. In this way, I believe, we can learn new lessons about the importance of building genuine family spirit in the groups of which we are a part.

When I reflect on the 2000-01 season, I have to give a lot of credit to my coaches, support personnel and, most of all, the players who demonstrated a genuine interest and respect for each other's differences. I am convinced that this respect is really what allowed them to develop the positive group cohesiveness necessary to achieve excellence during that magical season.

Promoting Acceptance and Respect

So how exactly did we do it?

For starters, I spoke with my coaches about the dormitory room assignments we would announce to the team before school began. We intentionally selected dorm facilities in which four players could live together in a two-bed-room apartment with a common living area, kitchen and bathroom. It's an arrangement that lets roommates get to know each other well and also provides space where team members and other students can hang out together. Single-bedroom dorm settings just don't provide an environment that fosters a sense of community.

Second, I found that the student-athletes on this 2000-01 team were one of the most inquisitive groups I've ever encountered. Their passion for learning was reflected in their scholastic records: ten of the 17 players on the team received a 3.0 or better grade point average during that academic year. But more than being good students, they were also genuinely interested in learning about each other, their cultural backgrounds and national issues.

And then there were the questions they asked during our practices. The sheer number of these questions frustrated me at first. Often I thought they might be questioning the authority and expertise of the coaches. I even suspect-ed that all those questions were being asked as a way to slow down the rigorous pace of our practices. But I quickly began to see that I was working with a group of intelligent players who wanted to better understand why we were asking them to do certain things. Once they understood what we wanted, they were able to execute plays with a greater sense of confidence and cohesiveness.

Multicultural experts say that these are just the kind of steps that foster acceptance and respect in diverse groups. The dorm set-up, for instance is obvi-ous: the experts say that "proximity" — that is, arranging situations in which people from different groups live and work together — is an important way to build a positive sense of community among people who are culturally different.

Another factor that helps generate positive group connections is the will-ingness of the leader to share power. This can be accomplished by allowing par-ticipants to raise questions about what the group is doing. While I admit I'm a "control freak," I've also learned that being patient and allowing my players to ask questions definitely contributed to a greater sense of purpose on the team. Moreover, when questions were asked I noticed that other players would offer suggestions and answers that helped their teammates better understand what we were trying to do. Intra-group discussion helps build positive connections among people from different cultural backgrounds, if it's done in a respectful and helpful manner.

Our sport counselors, Dr. Daniels and Dr. D'Andrea, have also helped our players deal with the inevitable frustrations and disagreements that occur within diverse groups — especially groups involved in such highly competitive and stressful endeavors. They call this "reframing their thinking." But whatever they call it, I can tell you that I was very impressed with the way it promoted a positive sense of community in the 2000-01 team. Here are some of the ways "the docs" accomplished this.

- They helped players combat inaccurate or negative interpretations of their teammates by exploring the flaws in some of their assumptions about those teammates.
- They provided plenty of supportive and positive comments to our players at practices.
- They helped the coaching staff see how cultural differences and learn ing styles can contribute to misunderstandings between coaches and players, and then suggested alternative approaches.
- They used various group activities to build an increased sense of cohesiveness. The Excellence Activity at the end of this chapter is one I found especially useful in helping us develop a genuine sense of family spirit.

By doing all of these things, we built a real community out of many disparate parts. What we may have lacked in overall basketball ability was compensated for in our ability to work together toward a common vision. We did this by respecting each others' differences, persevering during difficult times, remaining disciplined as individuals and as a group, and, most important, by committing to work together to build what we called "our family."

Building Family Spirit

The core value of family has always been at the center of my coaching philosophy. This has guided the way we want the players and coaches to relate to one another as a team. To foster a family spirit I invite all of the players to join my family for Thanksgiving, Christmas and Easter dinners. At Christmas dinner, our players sing carols while my wife, Joan, plays the piano. We have great fun with this tradition and usually call on one of the players or managers to sing a solo. It is truly heartwarming to see how the team comes together to share the holiday spirit as a family.

At our Christmas dinner in 2000, the players had an especially good time. I had made a bet with them that if anyone got a perfect 4.0 grade point average that semester, I'd let them shave my head. Much to my mixed emotions, Lane O'Connor met the challenge and earned a 4.0. Several players took turns using the clippers to collect on the bet. You will appreciate the sacrifice I made to help build our sense of family spirit if you knew how hard I've worked to grow my hair over the past 20 years or so.

I believe that our willingness to come together as a special "family" was a key factor in achieving our goals and realizing our vision. Together we gained a real respect for the power and potential of working within a respectful, caring and interdependent community. There's no question that the willingness of each individual — players, coaches, support personnel — to accept the unique roles asked of them at different times during the year contributed to our success.

My Commitment to Family

Many people see me as a tough-minded coach from the old school of coaching. They see a strong disciplinarian, red-faced on the sidelines over a referee's bad call or a player's lack of hustle. This old-school image is furthered by some of the brief sound bites and visual images of me that people pick up when they come to our games or watch us play on television.

I admit that I rant and rave on the sidelines from time to time. It's an expression of my passion and my competitive nature. Still, I'd like to think I'm more multidimensional than that. There's more to Riley Wallace than a big voice and a red face. There is, for example, my strong commitment to family. I highly value my role as father and husband, and I use this as a motivating force to create a special sense of connection and positive spirit among my players and coaches. This intense family commitment comes from the way my mother raised my brothers, sisters and me. On her deathbed she made us promise that the entire family would get together for a special time each year, when we were to celebrate our sense of connection, love and purpose as a family unit. My brothers, sisters and I have never failed to keep that promise, and I'm certain that we are better people for honoring my mother's wishes.

Strong family connections were especially important as my "economically challenged" family struggled with financial hardship. When we were young my three brothers and I learned that basketball could be our way out of these adverse circumstances. So we worked hard at a game we loved, seeing it as a way to advance ourselves in life. By my senior year in high school, I had received scholarship offers from 36 colleges. While this was a wonderful payoff for the time and energy I'd devoted to the game, I was not academically prepared to deal with the educational challenges I would face in college. In fact, in the second semester of my freshman year at Centenary, the woman in the Academic Registrar's office looked at my first semester grades, then looked up at me and said, "You should be digging ditches, not going to college!"

This was a serious wake-up call. I knew she was challenging me to make the changes necessary to become a successful student. And once I demonstrated a greater level of interest and motivation in my classes, I knew I could depend on professors and classmates to help me succeed in this new academic world. I also knew I could always turn to my brothers and sisters for moral support. The support we offered one another as we were growing up was instrumental in the strong values and work ethic we developed. Early in life we learned that hard work and positive family connections are key to overcoming difficult challenges.

Over the years I've learned important life lessons as a son, husband, parent and coach. As a result, I'm convinced that group success is linked to the way individuals demonstrate understanding, respect and interdependence with each other.

I have also learned that people are motivated to work harder when they have the opportunity to be part of a special community. Inevitably, they will sacrifice more, put personal interests and ambitions aside, and strive to help the group succeed in achieving its collective goals. The 2000-01 basketball team was a case in point: by working together, we were able to achieve unexpected levels of athletic, scholastic, professional and personal excellence, as individuals and as a special kind of family.

EXCELLENCE ACTIVITY

The Pulse

Here's an activity that our sport counseling and development specialists first used to promote a greater sense of unity among players and coaches during the 2000-01 season. First, the docs asked all of the players and coaches to join them in a circle. When people want to think of ways in which their group can achieve excellence, Dr. D'Andrea told us, it is useful to think of that group as a body. He observed that every body is made up of different anatomical systems — the skeletal system, the circulatory system, the respiratory system and so forth. For a body to operate at full potential, all of these systems must work together in unity. He went on to explain that for athletic teams, the most important organ in the body is the heart — the players' and coaches' collective desire and will to win.

Dr. Daniels then asked everyone to join hands, look down at the floor, and think about the heart of our team. She told us she was going to do something to the person next to her and that she wanted each person in turn to pass it around the circle. She then squeezed the hand of the person on her right and began counting the seconds out loud: "One and two and three and…"

The first time we did this, "the pulse" — the squeezing of hands one by one — petered out halfway around the circle. But by then everyone was enjoying the challenge of trying to get it around to all 18 people in the circle. So we tried it again and this time we made it in 28 seconds. Now the docs said they thought we could do much better and challenged us to do try again. This time we did it in 15 seconds. We did it again and got it down to eight seconds. One final try and we had passed the pulse around the circle in five seconds! Not only were we impressed with our improvement, we all got the point that the docs were trying to make: that with a lot of heart, we could truly work together as one body to achieve a common goal.

This simple group activity became a ritual we use regularly to increase our sense of purpose and positive connection with one another. It definitely works for us and can be easily used by other groups — in a classroom or at a staff retreat, for example. ●

PART TWO

COACHES AND PLAYERS

"I am because we are;

and because we are,

therefore I am."

— Proverb, Asanti tribe

CHAPTER FOUR

BOB NASH:
ANCHOR TO MY RUDDER

It was halftime at the WAC championship game and the adrenaline was pumping! Despite Tulsa's huge home court advantage, we were trailing by a margin of only 42-39, and I knew we could win this one. As I walked off the Reynolds Center court and entered the locker room, I focused on what I would tell our players. I read their faces, concerned yet hopeful. I knew we'd have to improve a few things, but I was confident we could pull it off if we stayed together and played the way we were capable of playing.

In the locker room I pointed out individual strengths and weaknesses during the first half. I reminded Carl English he should keep taking open shots — he was an impressive seven for 12 in the game — but I also told him to do a better job of getting the ball to our inside guys. I complimented Mike McIntyre on his defense, but reminded him he should try to draw fouls from the big Tulsa players by driving more to the basket. When I paused to collect my thoughts, I heard associate head coach Bob Nash say, "You have to stay focused, fellas. We can win this one. Just stay focused."

Then I directed my attention to Savo. I let him know he would have to stop fouling. We needed his offensive punch, and we needed him to play a much more effective defensive game. I turned to Mindaugas and told him what a gutsy first half he had played. I commended him for his rebounding work, a huge lift for us with Troy Ostler still out of the game with that badly re-injured ankle. As I considered specific offensive and defensive plays I wanted us to execute in the second half, I again overheard Coach Nash telling the players in that steady, soothing voice, "You have to keep your focus, fellas. Let's win this one." What a good combination Bob and I make, I thought. Me, the talkative coach who likes to give orders; and Bob Nash, the steady, calming influence who centers the players by reminding them to focus on the task at hand.

Sailing the Ship to Excellence

If the journey to excellence can be compared to a ship at sea, I see myself as the rudder that guides our course and Bob Nash as the ship's anchor.

Bob brings stability to our team during stressful times — in tiring practices and close games. This is not to suggest he isn't passionate about basketball. Fans who have watched him during close home games are very familiar with Bob's towel-waving, which always spurs the crowd into a supportive frenzy.

This ritual started back in the early '80s, when he and I worked with then-head coach Larry Little and the Rainbows still played at Honolulu's Neal S. Blaisdell Center. Coach Little got sick in the middle of an important game and had to leave the court. We recognized that the team needed all the help we could give to win this game against a strong opponent. With the Rainbows trailing late in the game, Bob stood and waved a towel to generate excitement and enthusiasm among the Blaisdell Arena crowd. This ploy served not only to get the fans into the game, it clearly inspired our players.

Whipping the home crowd into a frenzy is a time-tested way to provide an emotional lift in basketball. As the "sixth player," the crowd can definitely help a team find its energy reserves to overcome challenging situations. Since that night at Blaisdell, Bob's towel technique has paid big dividends in some important games.

But Coach Nash's biggest contribution for us has been to act as that anchor — a dependable source of stability. All groups can use an anchor during stressful times and while I don't mean to diminish the importance of enthusiastic coaches and players, I find it equally valuable to have people around who are calming influences. I've seen many college basketball players get caught up in the excitement of competition, then fail to execute their responsibilities effectively. This can cost them their focus, which can cost a team the game. Because it's only natural to temporarily lose concentration during stressful situations, it's all the more important to have individuals who can stay calm and focused. We all experience emotional letdown at times, and when this happens we can easily lose sight of our individual or group goals. This temporary loss of focus diminishes our potential to help our team or organization and lessens our ability to achieve excellence.

Losing our internal sense of balance affects all of us at different times. It can happen in parenting, in a stressful business deal, when teaching a group of rowdy students, or when trying to resolve a conflict with a neighbor. These are the times when leadership abilities are especially important. These are the times to settle down, get grounded, refocus on your vision, resolve the problem and accomplish the goal at hand. These are the anchoring leadership skills that Bob Nash has mastered in his life. By using his strengths as a calming force on our team, he helps our players remain centered, internally balanced and focused when striving to achieve excellence.

Maintaining Calmness by Managing Stress

Bob Nash can do this because he has learned how to incorporate stress management strategies in his own life. He began meditating regularly back in the early 1970s when he was a senior at the University of Hawai'i. While I see Bob as a mellow guy — especially for a basketball coach — he sees himself as a rather "hyper" person. Recognizing that these hyper tendencies might distract from his performance when he played basketball for UH, he began to study various meditative practices. One of his favorite meditation spots was the East-West Center gardens on the UH campus, a beautiful and tranquil environment away from the chaos of the dorms. There he could be balanced and centered, prepare himself emotionally and focus on team goals. This was especially important because Bob was such a hard-nosed, aggressive player; he led the Rainbows in personal fouls during the 1970-71 season. Through meditation, however, he was able to channel his intensity and aggressiveness into greater productivity and effectiveness. The following season he committed far fewer fouls and was the team's leading rebounder. His average 14.4 rebounds a game that year still stands as a school record.

Many athletes refer to their ability to stay calm while girding for intense competition as being "in the zone." Bob Nash used various techniques like transcendental meditation to help him get in that zone before games. He also developed an interest in the martial arts, particularly kung fu, which he studied at Aala Park in Honolulu in 1970. This interest in Eastern philosophies and meditative practices was further fueled by a trip to Hong Kong in 1982. There, Bob rose at dawn each day to join the hundreds of elderly Chinese gathered in Victoria Park to practice tai chi and other ancient spiritual exercises.

Coach Nash told me that the time he took to learn about meditation and the martial arts helped him develop a much higher level of mental and physical discipline. He believes this gave him an edge over the other players he faced in college and after he left UH, when he went on to play for the Detroit Pistons and the Kansas City Kings. Today Bob talks to our players about how meditation exercises enhanced his athletic performance — how they helped him remain calm, centered and oblivious to the crowds in packed arenas. And he points out that these Eastern practices have carried over into other aspects of his life, keeping him grounded when dealing with day-to-day stress.

Meditation is not my thing, which may be one reason I'm more excitable than Bob. Yet I know that psychologists and counselors use meditation in many ways: to help people gain calmness and clarity in pressure situations, to reduce hypertension, as a step in drug and alcohol rehab programs, and to help alleviate the anxiety students experience when faced with big exams or other academic challenges. Meditation is also being used more these days in sports performance enhancement programs. Many professional athletes now employ pre-game meditation exercises to help prepare for competition.

The Fabulous Five

Bob Nash is a strong leadership model for our student athletes for another important reason: he is committed to living a quality life. Obviously, a quality life has special requirements. One is nurturing a healthy body, mind and spirit. Another is setting realistic goals for a satisfying career with an adequate income. A third is enjoying the special feeling that comes from being part of a close-knit family. Bob has committed his life to successfully fulfilling all of these requirements.

Though we've worked together for 14 basketball seasons, I admit that Bob is not an easy person to know or understand. He is quiet and reserved. It has taken time for me to appreciate his attributes, but I think I now know him as well as anyone at the University of Hawai'i. Let me share some of the special qualities of this man, so that you can better know him — and the sense of dignity and integrity he shares with others.

Born in Georgia in 1950, Bob Nash moved to Hartford, Connecticut, with his family when he was in the ninth grade. He was a basketball stalwart at Hartford Public High School, where he earned All-American honors in his senior year. At San Jacinto Junior College in Pasadena, Texas, he was selected to the All-America Junior College second team in 1970, the year he averaged more than 22 points and 18 rebounds a game.

That was also the year that Bob transferred to the University of Hawai'i, where he was a member of one of the greatest basketball teams in Rainbow history. As a member of the revered "Fabulous Five," Nash played the next two seasons under head coach Red Rocha. During that time, the Rainbows racked up a 47-8 record and made the school's first-ever NCAA tournament appearance. No other University of Hawai'i basketball teams have had such victorious back-to-back seasons. With their commitment to excellence, the team captured the hearts and minds of Hawai'i's people — including many who'd never followed Rainbow basketball. Significantly, these athletes were not only winners on the court but also went on to achieve distinguished careers after their playing days ended.

During the glory days of the Fab Five, Bob Nash achieved a memorable level of excellence. Among the school records he still holds: most rebounds in a game (30 vs. Arizona State in 1971); most rebounds in a single season (361 during the 1971-72 season); and average rebounds per game (13.6). He also ranks seventh in career scoring average at the University of Hawaiʻi.

After the 1971-72 season, Bob was named a third team All-American by *The Sporting News*. He was selected honorable mention All-American by United Press International and the Associated Press. He was also named Most Valuable Player in the 1972 Aloha Classic tournament.

Following his college basketball career, Bob was picked seventh overall by the Detroit Pistons in the National Basketball Association's annual draft. He played in 71 games for Detroit from 1972-74 before joining the San Diego Conquistadors for 17 games during the 1974-75 season of the American Basketball Association. Bob also played in Sweden for two years, then returned to the NBA in 1977 with the Kansas City Kings, where he participated in 148 games over the next two seasons.

Playing in the pro ranks in the U.S. and Europe gave Bob a broad range of valuable experience to share with our team. He experienced the peaks of success and the depths of disappointment. He learned to be true to his dreams and to keep a strong work ethic. His passion for the game taught him to deal with the changes life can bring and led him to develop standards of excellence that serve him well to this day. Among other truisms, Bob tells his players that:

- "Nothing is laid out for you in life. You have to seize every opportunity. If you don't you only shortchange yourself."
- "Every situation in life presents change. More often than not that change is good. It's important not to resist life's changes, but to learn and grow from them."

Fulfilling His Educational Goal

Like Bob Nash, one way we can realize excellence is by leading balanced lives and by pursuing various goals that lead to a healthy mind and body, career success and a strong family. Our basketball program has introduced many services to help student-athletes develop skills for leading quality, well-rounded lives even as they participate in college athletics. And while these performance enhancement services are important ways to help a team, group or organization realize new heights of excellence, there's no substitute for a key role model. On our team that role model is Bob Nash.

Because Bob's main focus in 1972 was to realize his dream of playing professional basketball, he didn't complete the academic requirements necessary for graduation. But throughout his pro career in the U.S. and Europe, he never abandoned his goal of getting a college degree. As that career was winding down, he began taking courses during the summer months so that he could complete his student teaching requirements during the regular school year. In this way he completed all of his academic requirements and graduated with a bachelor's degree in education from the University of Hawai'i in 1984.

Bob's perseverance in achieving this personal goal makes him a perfect mentor for young athletes whose dreams of playing pro basketball override the importance of a degree. "When my playing days at UH were over," he recalls, "I knew I had a guaranteed salary to play professionally. But this isn't the case with most of our players. That's why it's so important that they expand their life options by completing their degrees before they embark on a professional basketball career."

Bob has convinced many of our players to stay in school until they graduate. For example, Johnny White, our point guard in the 1998-99 and 1999-00 seasons, had a strong desire to play basketball in Europe, but his mother wanted him to graduate from the University of Hawai'i. With Bob's encouragement, Johnny continued his studies after his playing eligibility ended, working toward a degree in liberal studies.

Communicating the value of a complete education holds a very special place on the Rainbow Circle of Excellence. Best of all, when our student-athletes receive their degrees, they're accomplishing a personal goal that will also help them achieve excellence in many other aspects of their lives.

Building Strong Family Connections

Bob Nash's commitment to family is another hallmark of his leadership abilities. Bob married the former Domelynne Lum in 1973. They have two children, Erika and Bobby, with whom Bob maintains the kind of positive connection that is vital to family interdependence. It comes as no surprise that one way Bob promotes strong family values is to share his love for athletics with his kids. Erika played volleyball in high school and college, and Bobby is a standout high school basketball player in Honolulu. Bob and his children often visit the gym early in the morning. "We like working out while the rest of the town is sleeping," he says. "We can get to the gym relaxed and focused, and it gives me time to connect with my kids without being distracted. And, of course, everyone's fresh that time of day."

Being "fresh" is important to Bob, who likes to say, "When you're green you grow!" It's one of many bits of advice he dispenses to help give his kids fresh perspective on their lives. Here's another: if Erika or Bobby didn't perform especially well in a game, he'd suggest they go for a long run to think about what they didn't do well. And he was always there to meet them at the end of the run to talk about the thoughts they had along the way.

"For Bob, every experience in life can be a lesson," says Domelynne. "He's always looking at what we can learn from any given situation. I know that's one reason he likes to sit close to the players on the bench during games. It gives him a chance to talk with them about why they think they were taken out of the game, and to review what they can do better next time."

Many times I've observed Bob as he spoke with players during a game. I can see him leaning on Phil Martin's shoulder as he talked to him about playing stronger defense against TCU during that first WAC tournament game. I can hear him calming Savo down, encouraging him to think more clearly about what he could do to help us win the championship. And I can hear him urging Haim and Troy to work harder and smarter in boxing out taller opponents to get more rebounds against Tulsa.

Promoting Excellence through Humor

Coach Nash is an effective communicator with a unique communications style. He has the gift of getting through to players even in the most stressful situations. To do this, he often uses his dry sense of humor as a tool to help them stay focused on our collective goals. During one especially rigorous practice, Savo was trying very hard to help Jeep Hilton learn one of our plays. When Jeep kept making the same mistake Savo grew so frustrated that he began to speak loudly in his native Serbian. Looking on with a deadpan expression, Bob turned to Savo and said, "Maybe the real problem here is that he doesn't understand Serbian!" Surprised, Savo walked away, laughing and shaking his head. After that I noticed that Savo resumed practice in a much improved state of mind, thanks to Bob's dry, disarming comment.

During another practice Coach Nash thought Phil Martin wasn't hustling. If one thing bothers Bob it's when players don't practice with a high level of intensity. Although he was clearly frustrated with Phil's lackadaisical play, Bob didn't ride him or raise his voice. Instead he approached him during a break in the action and said, "Phil, since you don't seem all that interested in working hard today, I just wanted to know if there was anything I could do to make you more comfortable!" Phil appreciated the sarcasm, along with Bob's real message, and as a result turned up the intensity several notches for the rest of the practice.

During a tough home game against Fresno State, a referee made what I felt was a bad call on one of our guys right before halftime. I decided to share my thoughts about this call in my usual passionate way — telling Coach Nash what the ref could do with his whistle, with my help. Hearing this, Bob turned to me with a straight face and said, "Coach, I'm not sure that would help the situation very much right now." Delivered with that serious expression, his remark caught me off guard and defused the situation. As the halftime buzzer sounded I thought, "He probably just saved me from a technical foul. For sure, he keeps my blood pressure down."

Some people use humor in degrading and disrespectful ways, hurting feelings and alienating people. But I have never heard Bob Nash use humor like that. His humor is motivating and to the point. It never diminishes another person's dignity. It's one of the many things I appreciate about Bob and another reason I find him such a special person.

With Dignity and Integrity

Dignity and integrity are personal values that are in short supply today. Maybe we need a refresher course in what these words actually mean. Back to my trusty American Heritage Dictionary, where I find that dignity means "to give honor to; to add to the status of; make seem important..." and integrity is defined as "strict personal honesty and soundness."

Both definitions describe to a tee the leadership traits I find most appealing in Bob Nash. Not surprisingly, these are traits that are essential for any team or organization in the pursuit of excellence. To these I would add his honesty and his ability to communicate a sense of honor, value and importance to others. A few examples from the 2000-01 season:

In January, after a 79-71 loss at home to the University of Texas at El Paso, I was quite unhappy with the way the team had played. In the locker room after the game I buttonholed several players and told them in no uncertain terms how I felt. One of those players was Mindaugas Burneika. I pointed out several mistakes and told him what he'd have to do to improve. After I left the locker room, Mindaugas became quite upset. His outburst about my comments was unproductive for him and for the teammates around him. That's when Coach Nash stepped in. "I want you to look at me when I say this," he told Mindaugas firmly. "Coach Wallace said what he did because he's trying to make you a better player. When you become a better player we will become a better team. Do you understand?" Mindaugas took that advice to heart and after that showed considerable improvement as the season progressed.

Bob communicates with players in ways that preserve their dignity, and makes them feel valued. I've learned a lot from him about the importance of communicating a genuine sense of dignity when interacting with others. It is safe to say that when you have a person like this in your organization, you are more likely to achieve a high level of excellence, especially during times of challenge and stress.

Coach Nash fosters a special family spirit among the players on our scout team, the guys who aren't on our starting roster. Their job is to learn all of the opposing teams' offensive and defensive plays and effectively execute them in practice. This helps our starters deal intelligently with the opposition in real game situations.

During the 2000-01 season, the scout team often changed. There were many reasons for this: multiple injuries at different times of the season, Haim's 22-game suspension, and my ongoing search for the best starting lineup. Consequently, most of the players saw duty on the scout team at some point during the season.

Bob took exceptional pride in his responsibilities with the scout team. "I want you to graduate from the scout team and challenge the starters!" he'd say to the players at practice. "I want them to feel you can take their jobs anytime — that they're walking on thin ice!" Developing a positive family spirit within the scout team kept these players motivated and competitive. The pride they felt underscored the special role they played on the team. Bob often reminded the entire team that we were winning games because of the scout team.

The family spirit Bob has helped develop also extends to the basketball program staff and even the players' parents. I watched how he connected immediately with Mahealani, our sports psychologists' toddler. Judy Daniels and Michael D'Andrea bring Mahealani to most of our practices and all of our games; she has been embraced by the whole team in a special way. And even after a tiring practice or an emotionally draining game, Coach Nash will go out of his way to spend a moment with her. "Come here, girl," he'll say. "I need a hug!" And he'll get one, too. Such gestures from Bob have helped Mahealani become another important member of our extended Rainbow Warrior family.

Bob communicates with players' parents regularly — chatting with them at length when they call to ask about their sons' progress, or sending personal notes during the holidays. What's more, he takes the time to learn about each new player's personal, academic and athletic history, whether he has personally recruited them or not.

The special kinship I have with Coach Nash results largely from our ability to work together in the interests of our student-athletes. Here's an example involving two of our key players — one like a stallion, with boundless energy and stamina, the other like an antelope, with different strengths and weaknesses. Together, Bob and I helped them both discover new dimensions of their personal power.

The Stallion and The Antelope

Since I was a kid I've been captivated by the power, energy and strength of the stallion. When I visited farms in Illinois I was in awe just watching one of these magnificent animals ambling across a field. While I was impressed with the stallion's physical strength, I was actually intimidated by its powerful spirit, vivid even in repose. I felt that if a stallion's power and strength were expressed in uncontrollable, unpredictable ways, something bad could happen.

As I grew up to play college ball then moved on to coaching, I realized how important it was to have a person on your team who could emulate the spirit of the stallion in competition. In fact, I will say that every successful basketball team has such a player, who demonstrates an almost tireless sense of energy and intensity on the court.

Predrag Savovic is our team's stallion. He comes to every practice and game ready to put all his physical power, strength and energy on the line. When we need a player to gallop to the basket — and hopefully draw a foul in the process — Savo is our man. When we need someone to take a hit from a strong, fast-moving opposing player, Savo is there. When we need someone to invigorate other players late in a game, Savo leads the charge.

In all my years of coaching I've known few players who exhibit as much drive, scoring power, athletic ability and passion for the game of basketball as Predrag Savovic. But I also know that if he's going to realize his full potential for greatness, he will have to learn to channel this passion and power toward a higher level of athletic and personal excellence. There were too many times I was forced to take him out of important games because his untamed spirit — the spirit of the stallion — simply got out of control. Too many fouls, too many forced shots.

Savo's childhood was far from normal. He grew up in Yugoslavia, a country devastated by war. There's no question that the death and destruction he encountered in this ravaged part of the world contributed to the fervor he exhibits today. People say Coach Nash showed the same spirit of the stallion when he was younger. I've been told that Bob played with "reckless abandon" early in his college basketball career. But his subsequent ability to control and balance his own stallion tendencies now make him a valuable mentor to Savo, helping him become more focused and disciplined in his game. As head coach, I also saw it as part of my job to help Savo balance the energy and intensity of the stallion with the wisdom and pace of the antelope. For a model of the antelope, we turned to Savo's friend and teammate, Nerijus Puida.

The Ways of the Antelope

The antelope presents a counterpoint to the stallion. While its physical power is clear, it is the antelope's alertness and sense of cooperation that distinguishes it from the stallion. Rather than using sheer power to survive, antelopes seem more calmly attentive to their surroundings. They also work more closely with others in their herd.

Nerijus Puida was our team's antelope during the 2000-01 season. He was alert to what was happening around him, communicated well with his teammates, and used his athletic skills and mental acuity to do the right thing at the right time in game situations. These, by the way, are traits that Savo could use to balance his passion and to realize higher levels of excellence.

I remember Nerijus' first year as a Rainbow Warrior, when his cooperative spirit often led him to pass the ball even when he had a wide-open shot. Unfortunately, other teams began to recognize this unselfish act as a weakness and were able to adjust their defenses accordingly.

Nerijus' cultural background and experiences influenced his antelope spirit. He grew up in a small rural town in Lithuania near the Russian border. Life was hard for Nerijus and his family, but the experience was made considerably easier by the close-knit sense of community that often develops in rural areas. From it, Nerijus acquired a strong appreciation for teamwork and interdependence with others.

Although I highly respect Nerijus' team-oriented sense of interdependence, I recognized that I would have to encourage him to balance his antelope spirit with the energy of the stallion. Near the end of the 1999-00 season I pulled him aside and told him he'd have to develop a more aggressive offensive mindset if he really wanted to take his game to the next level. While I needed him to maintain the solid composure that would help our team achieve excellence, I knew we would also benefit if Nerijus let his "stallion" out from time to time.

Coach Nash offered to help Nerijus work on specific ways to tap into his stallion spirit and become a more balanced player. The quickest way, Bob figured, was to help him develop more confidence in his shooting ability. With Bob's encouragement, Nerijus spent hours practicing his outside shot during the summer before the 2000-01 season, and consequently developed a much more accurate shooting touch. In the process, he gained the self-confidence necessary to balance his deliberate and team-oriented spirit with a more aggressive offensive style — including a willingness to shoot and score in game situations. This new, improved approach to his game was exactly what we needed from Nerijus to help our team realize its vision of excellence in the 2000-01 season. The improvements in his game and his confidence were a direct result of his conversations with me and of the supportive leadership style of Bob Nash.

The kind of leadership that Coach Nash provides often goes unnoticed in our busy world. I strongly believe we can all learn a great deal about excellence and effective living by observing people like Bob. I know his family benefits from the sound leadership he demonstrates at home, and our players, coaches and support personnel clearly value the dignity and integrity he shares with them. From my perspective, the world would be a much better place if there were more Bob Nashes around.

EXCELLENCE ACTIVITY

Managing Stress with Meditation

Because meditation is a useful way to help people achieve excellence in a broad range of applications, you might want to use it to enhance your own performance. It can improve the quality of your life by helping you deal more effectively with daily stress and increasing your personal level of peace and satisfaction.

The meditative experience produces a level of consciousness that can best be described as a state of calmness and clarity, both of which are empowering and pleasurable. A person can meditate in many different ways. Popular techniques include transcendental meditation, yoga breathing, breath meditation and other, more sophisticated, approaches.

Breath meditation is an easy way to gain control over stress-related reactions. The technique requires only ten or 20 minutes a day and involves four basic steps:

- First, find a quiet spot where you'll be free from interruptions.
- Next, take a comfortable sitting position, close your eyes and begin to consciously shift your attention from the outside world to your own even breathing. Concentrate on the air going into your lungs and out again. As you focus your attention in this manner, continue to con centrate on your breathing patterns for a few minutes. If your mind begins to wander, simply refocus your attention on your breathing.

- Third, after focusing on your breathing for a few minutes, begin to silently count "one" as you inhale through your nose and mouth. As you begin to exhale, say to yourself "and." At the next inhalation continue your count — "two" — and as you exhale, silently count "and." When you've counted to four in this manner, begin the count over again, following this procedure in a relaxed manner for ten or 15 minutes, or as long as you feel comfortable doing so.
- Finally, open your eyes slowly and sit for about a minute to reflect on your feelings. It's important to remember that distracting thoughts usually occur when you begin practicing meditation. Don't get frustrated; it's normal. Try this several times over a period of a few days to see if meditation is right for you. ●

Associate head coach Bob Nash (*right and above, far right*) stirs up the home crowd with his trademark towel waving.

Above: Assistant coaches Jackson Wheeler (*top left*) and Scott Rigot.

Left: Shifty point guard A.C. Carter led the Rainbows to post-season tournaments two years in a row, then went on to the NBA to start for the Miami Heat.

Mindaugas Burneika, Lithuania

Predrag "Savo" Savovich, Montenegro

Mike McIntyre, California

Phil Martin, Ontario

Nerijus Puida, Lithuania

Carl English, Newfoundland

Haim Shimonovich, Israel

David "Jeep" Hilton, New York

CHAPTER FIVE

JACKSON WHEELER: OVERCOMING THE ODDS

Through all the excitement of beating Tulsa and winning the WAC Tournament, I knew something was missing. That "something" was assistant coach Jackson Wheeler, who was in San Francisco that week on a recruiting trip. Jackson plays several special roles on our team. One of our two assistant coaches, he is recognized nationally as a successful recruiter of junior college basketball players. Two of his big-name recruits to the University of Hawai'i were Trevor Ruffin (1992-94) and Anthony "A.C." Carter (1996-98). In 1994 Ruffin helped Hawai'i win its first-ever WAC Tournament title, which led to an NCAA tournament berth for the first time in 22 years. A.C., who went on to start for the Miami Heat, propelled the Rainbows into the national spotlight by leading them to back-to-back, 20-plus-win seasons and consecutive trips to the National Invitational Tournament in '96 and '97.

In addition to his recruiting duties, Jackson plays other essential roles on our team. He is a friend, mentor, academic counselor and tutor, as well as a personal adviser and close confidant for many of our student-athletes. The bond he develops with our players is special. He has a real knack for empathizing with our players, especially the ones from troubled backgrounds or those experiencing personal difficulties in Hawai'i.

Much of Jackson's empathy stems from the dramatic hardships and tragedies he has endured himself. In a very genuine way, Coach Wheeler understands other people's frustration and pain because he's been there. His powerful story reminds us that one can learn to live an effective life — and achieve personal and professional excellence — despite extreme difficulties in childhood, adolescence and young adulthood. When you read about his life experiences, I think you'll agree when I say that Jackson is truly a mountain of endurance. You'll better understand why I feel so fortunate to have him as an assistant coach. More than that, you'll know why I am proud to have him as a friend.

Growing Up In a Troubled Family

Jackson Wheeler was born in 1959 in San Luis Obispo, California, the oldest child in a family of two boys and two girls. His father was a car salesman;

his mother a nurse's aide. Because both parents were alcoholics, violence was a common occurrence in the Wheeler household. According to Jackson, his father was particularly abusive, both physically and verbally, and was neither a positive nor stable force in the home.

Substance abuse and violence finally led to his parents' divorce when Jackson was 11 years old. Despite his father's problems with alcohol and his history of abusive behavior, the divorce court ruled that Jackson and his brother would live with their father, while his sisters stayed with their mother.

The following year, however, his father was imprisoned for illegal money handling at the California car dealership where he worked, so Jackson returned to live with his mom. Monthly welfare checks, food stamps and other government funded programs were the main source of family income. As a result, Jackson and his siblings found themselves living in run-down hotels and were even homeless for months at a time.

Jackson's relationship with his mother and stepfather was stormy through most of his teenage years. Over time, her substance abuse, money troubles and other personal problems made life unbearable for the young man. As the oldest child in the family, he bore the brunt of the abuse. He began looking for a way out of this dysfunctional family environment that was causing so much hurt, confusion, depression and anger. In despair, he asked his best friend's parents if he could live with them. They agreed, and he received approval from the California Social Services Department to change families when he was 16.

Shortly after Jackson moved in with his new family, his father was released from prison. But it wasn't long till the senior Wheeler was in trouble again; this time he went underground to avoid going back to jail. Jackson knew he'd probably never see his father again. He did, however, stay in touch with his brothers and sisters, who continued to live with his mother. But his brief visits home only reminded him how lucky he was to have been adopted by his new family.

"The lack of family stability I experienced as a child and teenager made me not care much about studying," Jackson recalls. "As a result I was a below-average student and not very motivated at school. But one of the best things I did in high school was play on the basketball team for a coach who took a personal interest in me. Although I didn't fully understand it at the time, the way he cared for me, encouraged me and pushed me to do better in life was very important in giving me the confidence I needed to move ahead. Coach Sal Cardinale had a very positive effect in my development. He brought a much-needed sense of stability into my life at a critical time."

The attention and encouragement paid off big-time: Jackson graduated from high school, then went on to Marymount College in Kansas on a basketball scholarship.

Losing a Loved One

Wheeler met his first wife in college. "Cindy was a stabilizing force in my life," Jackson says. "She helped me find direction and get organized. She also helped me understand the importance of leading a moral and respectful life. And she helped me think about and clarify my goals. She was my shining light."

Cindy and Jackson were married upon graduation from Marymount in 1982. They both entered graduate school in a small college in Nebraska. Wheeler speaks proudly of her ability to set financial goals and save money, and to help him develop a greater sense of financial responsibility. As a result, they saved enough to buy a condominium.

Cindy also helped him achieve excellence in his educational pursuits. He was motivated to graduate with a master's in sports management, while Cindy completed her requirements for a master's degree in theater.

This positive turn in life was given another boost in 1985, when Jackson got his first college basketball coaching opportunity at Highland Community College in Highland, Kansas. The job marked the beginning of a career well-suited to such a caring individual. Yet the excitement and promise of the good life was tragically interrupted when Cindy was killed in an auto accident by a drunk driver in the summer of 1987, while Coach Wheeler was out of town at a basketball camp.

Shook to the core of his being, Jackson nevertheless returned to coaching at Highland Community College. With three top junior college basketball players on the roster, he led his team to a conference championship. Then, in the summer of 1988, he accepted the assistant coaching job at St. Louis University. Besides the normal responsibilities of an assistant coach, Jackson was designated the main recruiter on the St. Louis staff. While he was there, the team went to the National Invitational Tournament Final Four two years in a row. Much of this success was attributed to Coach Wheeler's ability to recruit talented players. As a result, he developed a national reputation as a top recruiter.

Despite his success, the void left by Cindy's death was huge. But Jackson had made a conscious decision not to turn to drugs or alcohol to ease his pain. Instead he found constructive ways of dealing with his loss. In doing so, he showed that, even in the face of great odds and adversity, we can still make the choices that let us go on to lead effective and satisfying lives.

Finding New Rainbows

After two years at St. Louis University, Jackson was ready for a break. He had heard through the grapevine that I might be seeking another assistant coach, so he flew to Hawai'i to apply. He began working in our program as a graduate assistant, then moved into our relatively new, full-time assistant coaching position with the men's basketball team in 1989. The more I worked with him, the more I sensed something special about Jackson Wheeler. A hard worker and a recruiter with a great track record, Jackson also showed a genuine sense of caring for others, especially people who had lived difficult lives. Let me give you an example.

A familiar sight around the UH athletic facility is the man who digs through trash barrels looking for aluminum cans, which he sells for recycling. While most people look right past him, Jackson not only stops and talks with the man but even brings him empty aluminum cans from home. "I really respect this guy," Jackson explains, "for trying to make it in life the only way he may know how. I know other people probably look down on him for digging in the trash, but what I see is a guy doing something positive, who works hard every day for what he has. I know what it's like to come to work every day, fighting an uphill battle just to keep yourself together. Maybe I can relate to that man in a personal way that other people can't."

Any group would benefit from this kind of compassion and empathy — the ability to effectively relate to people whose lives have been such a struggle. These are the kinds of traits I see in Jackson Wheeler — qualities that make me glad he chose to join the Rainbow Warrior family.

After he moved to Hawai'i, Jackson found a new rainbow — and pot of gold — when he met his current wife, Lael Lee. He acknowledges that many of Lael's qualities remind him of Cindy. She, too, is a calm and stable presence in his life. But he also fell in love with Lael for her own unique qualities — her strong work ethic, for example, and an uncompromising willingness to assert her views. Because Lael isn't much interested in sports, she helps him keep his job separate from his home life. And that makes it easier, he points out, to direct his love and attention to this woman who is now his life partner.

Jackson's "Unexpected Happenings"

Jackson Wheeler's story shows how a person can use the unexpected to create new and positive ways of living an effective life and achieving excellence. Naturally, Jackson didn't expect to grow up in a dysfunctional family where violence was the norm. He didn't even expect to graduate from high school. And he certainly didn't expect to marry a woman who would die in a senseless auto accident. He probably didn't expect to become a basketball coach on an island in the middle of the Pacific Ocean. But Jackson has managed to find personal nourishment in all of these unexpected experiences.

Jackson's unusual background has clearly influenced his coaching style. When he approaches players who are having trouble meeting challenges, he shares his coaching and life philosophy like this:

"When I encounter players with big problems, I can relate to them in a really personal way. I can tell them a little bit about my own life to let them know that I understand where they're coming from. I remind them that everyone has tragedies and obstacles in life, but that some are worse than others. I emphasize that how an individual deals with his challenges ultimately defines the person he becomes. I try to help them see the possible positive side of dealing with negative situations, just as I've done in my own life."

The Players: Lessons in Resilience

I wanted to share Jackson's story to show how one member of our team uses different components of the Rainbow Circle of Excellence to lead an effective life. But the proof, of course, is in the results. The success of Jackson's approach is evident in the way our coaching staff has been able to help players with their own rocky histories. Consider the story of Bosko Radovic, and what he had to deal with in his first year as a Rainbow Warrior. Freshly arrived from Montenegro, Yugoslavia, in the summer of 2000, Bosko had to cope not only with culture shock but also with the traumatic experience of being assaulted and robbed en route to the States. Nevertheless, he began adjusting to his new life in Hawai'i and showed signs of being the fine player we hoped he would be as he learned our play system. By scoring 14 points in the first half, he was responsible for keeping us in a game we played at UCLA. But then his season was abruptly cut short when he broke his leg in a freak accident in practice. An injury like this is obviously a big psychological — not to mention physical — hurdle. But not only did Bosko recover fully, he became a stronger person through sheer determination and resilience.

Or consider the trials and tribulations of Todd Fields. A player who has suffered years of leg injuries, Todd has demonstrated the physical and mental grit that enable a player to compete at the Division I level. But what's even more admirable is the way he dealt with the death of his father at the start of the 1999-2000 season. The unexpected event renewed his passion to excel and to realize his dream of graduating from college. As one of the most respected play-

ers on the team, he always pushed his teammates to realize their athletic potential by challenging them to improve their skills. What's more, he did an unusually good job of fostering a special sense of family spirit among our players and
coaches with his good humor and enthusiastic disposition.

Todd kept his level of enthusiasm high throughout the season because,
as he put it, "that's what my dad would want me to do. When I was hurt or felt
down during the year, I reminded myself that I was doing it for my dad. That
was all I needed to get through the hard times. I knew he was watching me and
I wanted to make him proud."

David "Jeep" Hilton's life experiences were just as dramatic. Like Jackson,
Jeep grew up in an abusive and alcoholic family environment. At age 15 he
began to rebel against his mother, who then kicked him out of the house. Much
of his time was spent wandering the streets of New York City, sleeping on park
benches or in the subway on rainy nights. Still, he kept moving forward with
his life, and along the way he met Lilabet Foster.

Lilabet is an Academy Award-nominated producer, who was filming a
documentary on the problems of the homeless called "Soul in the Hole" when
she met Jeep. She helped get him into a group home living situation and a Boys'
Club and eventually helped him enroll in the prestigious Hyde School, a
Connecticut boarding facility. At Hyde Jeep finally found the stability that
helped him develop a sense of confidence — socially, academically and athletically. He was even able to overcome a lifelong stuttering problem. His early
hardships taught him many unforgettable life lessons. Says he:

"I realize that no matter how hard things are, they'll eventually get better. The difficult times are all just preparation for what will come in the future,
and they'll help me become stronger. In life, when things don't go our way, we
often tend to get mad at the situation. But I've learned from my experiences
that you can't give up. You have to keep fighting back, work harder and learn to
accept the difficult times."

Jeep says he looks up to two women who have been important in his
life. One is his grandmother, Novelle Hilton, who worked hard to overcome
poverty and a lack of education to become a homeowner. Another is Lilabet
Foster, who has become a kind of surrogate parent. When she was interviewed
by Roger Rubin for a story in the *New York Daily News*, she said about Jeep, "It's
hard to describe what we have gone through in our relationship because it has
changed over the years. It started out almost as parent and child but now it is
like we are friends. He has developed and matured a lot. He gives me advice
now." Jeep's story shows how anyone can achieve excellence in life by persevering to overcome long odds.

Carl English: Childhood Tragedies

The player's story I find most moving is that of Carl English. Carl was born in St. John's, Newfoundland, in the winter of 1981 and spent his formative years in Branch Saint Mary's, a small Canadian fishing village of just 500 people. He was the second youngest of five boys. In this remote township almost everyone boasted a working class background.

Carl was five years old when he heard a commotion downstairs in his home. In starting the family's wood-burning stove to heat the house, his father had caught fire himself and the blaze was spreading fast. Carl and his brothers had only a few minutes to escape. His nine-year-old brother, Bradley, jumped out a bedroom window; his eldest brother, Peter, managed to escape out the back door and raised a ladder to a window on the second floor. That ladder became a life-saving escape route for Carl and his brothers Kevin and Michael.

The house was quickly destroyed but what was worse, Carl's parents were severely burned. Despite desperate medical efforts, Carl's mother died in the hospital six days after the fire, and his father three days after that.

Finding a New Family Spirit

Fortunately, Carl's aunts and uncles provided tremendous support to the five brothers. But because none of them could care for all five boys together, the family was split up. Bradley moved in with his mother's sister, and the other three brothers went to live with another aunt and uncle. Carl was taken in by his Aunt Betty and Uncle Junior McGrath, who had three sons and a daughter.

Betty and Junior worked hard to help the boy feel a part of their family by providing a stable and loving environment. Yet, Carl still vividly recalls the confusion and sadness he felt after his parents' deaths. He talks about not fully realizing what was going on, how he cried a lot because "I missed my mom and dad and wanted them to be with me. I blamed myself a lot for their deaths even though I know that doesn't make sense. I remember wondering why they didn't take me with them. I remember being confused as to why they weren't around anymore."

While Carl grew close to his Aunt Betty and Uncle Junior, he says that it "just wasn't the same as being with my real mom and dad. I remember how my relatives told me how much I was like my mom and dad, but I didn't really understand what they meant. I think I was too young to know them and to remember their qualities. I really missed being able to know them better."

The love and security provided by Aunt Betty and Uncle Junior helped Carl develop new strengths to cope with his loss. "The whole experience made me a much stronger person," he says now, "even if I was just a young kid when it happened. Having to go through something like that prepared me for the other punches in life. Not too much could bring me down after I lost my parents in the fire."

Basketball – Another Source of Strength

Basketball became a way out of Carl's frustration and loneliness: "I found that when I played basketball with intensity, I could put all the problems aside and feel better afterward too." He watched the game on television from an early age and played basketball for hours on end with his cousins. Because they were older, he was forced to push harder to develop his competitive skills. The closest gymnasium was a half-hour's drive away, so Carl put up a basket at home when he was ten — "a great place to play with my brothers, cousins and friends."

By the time he entered sixth grade, he had developed a real passion for basketball and was already recognized as a fine young player. Still, people looked at his skinny frame and wondered how far he could really go in the game. "In elementary school I dreamed about playing basketball in high school and college," he recalls. "I kept this dream alive and knew that one day I'd prove the doubters wrong."

In high school Carl was taken under the wing of basketball coach Gord Pite, who taught him new skills and new ways to think about the game. Carl soon learned that Pite was much more than just a sports mentor: "Coach Pite was a real father figure who was able to help me develop into the person and player I am now."

As a junior in high school, Carl averaged a whopping 50 points a game. Now the doubters were few and far between. Recognizing that Carl couldn't develop his full potential in such a small community, Coach Pite, Uncle Junior and Aunt Betty made arrangements for a transfer to much larger St. Thomas Aquinas High School in Ontario. As it happened, Carl's hopes were temporarily dashed when the St. Thomas Aquinas teachers called a strike and the basketball season was canceled. But just as he was contemplating packing his bags and heading back to Newfoundland, he was invited to play for the prestigious Prep Stars Canada team in the spring of 1998. When Carl helped this team reach the state tournament, college recruiters in the U.S. began taking notice.

Invited to a basketball camp in New Jersey that summer, Carl was scrutinized closely by scouts and recruiters. He was rated as the best player at the camp, and word of his talents soon traveled all the way to University of Hawai'i assistant coach and recruiter Scott Rigot. When Carl scored a game-high 42 points at an all-star game in Philadelphia against talented Division I prospects,

Scott began courting Carl to enroll at UH. He agreed to join us as a student-athlete in the fall of 1999.

New Challenges Ahead

When Carl arrived in Hawai'i for the fall semester, he already knew something was wrong with his left ankle. Soon he learned that corrective surgery would be necessary if he was going to make it at the college level. And so he sat out the 1999-2000 season, though he still kept his full four years of eligibility. During this major setback, his vision of becoming a successful Division I player never waned. He continued to share his passion for basketball, working enthusiastically with his teammates during practices and games, even if it was from the sidelines. His positive, easy-going interpersonal style contributed a great deal to our family spirit, that essential requirement for achieving excellence and realizing collective goals.

Carl was able to maintain his positive disposition despite the many miles he had put between his home and the people he loved. His loneliness in Hawai'i was compounded by the ankle surgery and the culture shock that many student-athletes find upon arrival in the Islands. Nevertheless, he met all these challenges with an impressive determination.

But when Carl returned to Newfoundland the following summer vacation to spend time with his family, another tragedy struck. One of his favorite pastimes was fishing with his brothers, cousins and Uncle Junior. One lovely afternoon, his uncle took Carl and a few other people fishing in his boat. Afterward, as they were unloading their catch, Uncle Junior grabbed his chest and cried out in pain. Carl, standing closest to him, held his uncle in his arms while he died. "Carl" was his last word. "All I could hear him say was my name in a very soft voice," Carl recalls. "It was like he was trying to say goodbye to me. He was my biggest fan and supporter. He knew playing college ball was something I dreamed of doing, and he was there to help me achieve that dream. His death was another difficult blow to deal with. But now I know I have three people watching over me and rooting for me when I play."

Gaining Strengths from Personal Loss

Like others who experience personal tragedy, Carl English has learned a lot about his inner strengths and the importance of personal relationships. He treasures the sacrifices made by his aunts and uncles to keep his brothers together. Their positive family spirit helped him deal with the lonely, sad and confusing emotions he had about the deaths of his parents. What's more, Carl has clearly seen how positive results can come from the most negative events. By dealing with life's tragedies, he has become a more independent person and gained a tremendous amount of self-confidence and resolve: "These awful things have made me more determined than ever to realize my dreams."

Carl, Jeep, Todd and Bosko have dealt with personal tragedy and loss in different ways. In the process, each has (1) defined his own character, and (2) nurtured a strong sense of personal pride, discipline and passion for life. Each of these players has taught me much about the power of resilience and why this component of the Rainbow Circle of Excellence is so important in the pursuit of excellence.

EXCELLENCE ACTIVITY

Community Service

The pursuit of excellence also takes us out into the community, as we strive to be responsible, contributing citizens. In our basketball program, we promote this by asking our players to participate in community service projects throughout the school year. In this way our student-athletes gain a greater sense of responsibility for helping maintain the welfare of our society. For example, they visit local schools to give anti-drug and anti-violence presentations and to discuss the importance of getting an education. I've also arranged for our players to visit sick children in local hospitals during the holiday season. Such service projects are small but important gestures that promote a positive sense of family spirit among our team and members of the community around them.

Research shows that, besides providing much-needed help to schools, churches and communities, people who participate in such activities also benefit personally in a number of ways. This includes feeling better about themselves (increasing their self-esteem), developing new friendships (expanding their social support networks) and developing a more positive and optimistic view of the future.

Having seen the beneficial impact that our student-athletes make in the community — as well as the increased sense of pride, respect and responsibility they earn for themselves — I strongly encourage you to make a similar commitment to do something constructive for your own community. Volunteer to help out at a homeless shelter. Set time aside to tutor a youngster in need at a nearby school. Talk about your job during a school's career week. Offer assistance on your church's next community project. Give yourself a definite time frame — one month, for instance — to get started, and then get out and do it! ●

CHAPTER SIX

SCOTT RIGOT:
INTERNATIONAL AMBASSADOR

Assistant Coach Scott Rigot is an intense teacher of basketball. In fact, Scott does just about everything with a highly energetic sense of purpose, thought, and emotion. He throws himself fully into his work, fueled by his passion for basketball and his great desire to succeed.

Given this level of intensity, it didn't surprise me when I saw tears in his eyes as the final seconds of the WAC Championship game ticked away. He was truly ecstatic as he hugged players, coaches and anyone else within reach. The look on his face said it all: jubilation, pride and the tremendous sense of accomplishment that comes with achieving excellence over the rainbow. The time and effort he had devoted to helping our players learn new strategies had paid off. We were the champions of the Western Athletic Conference and Scott's role as a teaching tactician was an important factor.

The Importance of the Tactician

When I call Coach Rigot a "tactician" I use the dictionary definition: "A person skilled in the planning and execution of specific tactics to achieve an intended purpose." Another definition of this term is: "A person proficient in thinking about strategies that produce positive outcomes." Scott is clearly all of this and more. Many times he has come to my office to talk about different offensive strategies that would complement the specific strengths of our players. As a result I've come to respect his ability to think in creative ways. He's especially gifted in explaining how a specific player might effectively maneuver to score or rebound.

Because I liked Scott's ideas, I agreed to try them out during the 2000-01 season. I added several of his suggestions to our offensive play book, and they helped our players develop the response-ability they needed to meet the challenges of different opponents during the season. Scott's teaching skills were particularly valuable to a number of our smaller players — Nerijus Puida, Savo Savovic, Mike McIntyre and Carl English. He helped them develop their basketball potential by learning different nuances of the game in general and their positions in particular.

For instance, Scott would work with Carl in practice, helping him learn to outmaneuver an opponent by going to the basket in a different direction. And during the championship game in Tulsa, Scott was constantly reminding Carl how to more effectively run our offense. Each time he did this Carl's confidence went up a notch or two. Near the end of regulation, I called for him to run a specific play as the final seconds ticked off. We needed a basket to tie the game and go into overtime. I thought I detected a bit of Scott Rigot in Carl when he saw that the play was going awry and, instead, drove to the basket himself for a tough, off-balance lay-up with only four seconds left.

What a critical basket! Yet, I also have to credit Coach Rigot for spending so many hours in practice teaching tactics to Carl and our other players. His instructional style not only helped our team learn more effective ways of executing plays, it encouraged self-confidence in each individual player. Along with Bob Nash and Jackson Wheeler, Scott did so much to help our players develop a clear understanding of what we could achieve if we continued to use all the elements of the Rainbow Circle of Excellence.

We weren't the only ones who noticed the team's progress as the season unfolded. After we eliminated defending champion Fresno State in the second game of the WAC Tournament, FSU Coach Jerry Tarkanian said he'd noticed big differences in our team. "The changes you made in your offensive game and the way your players have developed," Tark told me, "have really made a difference since the last time we played you." (Fresno State had beaten us decisively back in February by a score of 86-63.) Then he paid us the ultimate compliment: "At this point in the year, you're probably playing the best half-court game in college basketball." Those few words spoke volumes about our teamwork throughout the season, and I genuinely appreciated the role our tactician played in helping us achieve excellence on that memorable March night in Tulsa.

The Tactician's Role

How does Coach Rigot use his skills as a teaching tactician? Some people in basketball would call him our "X and O man." He is forever outlining new plays on his clipboard with those standard symbols for offensive and defensive players. He uses his diagrams to help players visualize new ways of thinking about the plays they're expected to execute in practice and in games. Coach Rigot is a big believer in diagrams and other visual tools.

"I'm a visually-oriented teacher," he explains. "I think players learn much better when they can get a picture in their minds of the new things I'm trying to teach them. I don't think many people learn much about the game of basketball unless they can actually see what they're supposed to be doing in their heads before they execute a move or a play. So I use a lot of diagrams to explain what we want our players to do and show them film of our opponents' games to see in their minds exactly what they have to do to beat them."

Personally, I think it's oversimplifying to describe Scott as simply our X and O man. When Scott works with our players he helps them develop new and sophisticated ways of thinking about themselves and their athletic environment. That is, he helps them develop new mental models of the game of basketball. Then he works with them to put those models into practice, with an eye toward game situations. This is the essence of a great teacher.

To achieve excellence in life, we all need great teachers who can:
- Help us create new ways of thinking about our endeavors
- Help us acquire the skills we need to meet challenges
- Inspire us to work hard to realize our untapped potential for excellence

Based on that, in fact, all of our coaches are great teachers. Bob Nash's coaching style not only helps our players learn more effective ways of playing basketball, it also encourages them to think about the importance of leading a disciplined, balanced life. Jackson Wheeler's empathy enables him to teach from the heart, making the personal connections that motivate our players to remain strong in the face of difficult challenges. Using a more visually-oriented and animated teaching style, Coach Rigot always has a new perspective to share.

An Effective Communicator

Scott, who joined the UH men's basketball program in 1999, knows how to communicate. This is critical to his success, not only as a teaching tactician but also as a recruiter. Scott began his coaching career at the University of South Carolina in 1986, working as an assistant coach under head coach George Felton until 1990. During his stay at South Carolina, he recruited several key players who helped the Gamecocks achieve an unprecedented level of success: three consecutive winning seasons, a Top 10 Recruiting Class in 1988 and a post-season National Invitational Tournament bid in 1989. At South Carolina Scott also met and married his wife, Renee; the couple now has a daughter, Natalie Renee.

Before starting at the University of South Carolina, Scott spent 16 years with the Five-Star Basketball Camp, where high school, college and international players develop their basketball skills and knowledge. The camp also provides an excellent training ground for individuals who want to coach and teach at the college level. Scott began attending this camp in his first year of college.

His experience at the Five-Star Basketball Camp was one of the reasons I asked him to join the Rainbow family. Today his reputation as an effective recruiter extends beyond U.S. borders and his recruiting efforts have helped us become a stronger, deeper team. As a result of his work, we've enrolled such key players as Carl English and Phil Martin from Canada, Bosko Radovic from Yugoslavia and Haim Shimonovich from Israel.

There are many things I like about Scott's approach to recruiting student-athletes to Hawai'i. Above all is his commitment to academic excellence. He tells his recruits that "excellence means more than just winning games," and he helps provide the support they need to graduate from UH. We want our recruits to know from day one that they're expected to excel personally and academically as well as athletically.

Much has been made of the many players we have from so many different countries. According to NCAA reports, the 2000-01 University of Hawai'i team was the most culturally diverse college basketball team in the nation, with seven international players. Davidson and Niagara Universities each had six international players on their rosters, and several other schools had five each. And following that season, our team actually increased in diversity, as we signed recruits from several other countries including France, Nigeria and South Africa.

How did our team become so multinational? Much of the credit goes to Coach Rigot, whose parents are of Serbian and French ancestry. He grew up in Pittsburgh in a "working-class ethnic neighborhood," he says, which was home to many families from Europe.

"Growing up around so many people from such different backgrounds," he explains, "I think I was able to develop an openness and sensitivity to cultural differences at an early age. While many people seem to think their own cultural group is better than any other, I was fortunate to grow up in a situation that helped me be less ethnocentric. Many Americans have negative stereotypes about people from other countries, especially non-English speakers, but I try to look for the positive things about these people. When I'm with someone who has difficulty speaking English, I work harder to try to understand what he's saying. In this way, I often find something new and interesting about that person.

"I've also learned that using humor can be a good way to connect with people from different backgrounds. When I'm in a situation with people from different countries, I often find myself making jokes about my own cultural background as a way to break the ice and help them feel more comfortable. Humor can be such a useful tool. I use it a lot when I'm trying to recruit a player from another country or as I'm building a relationship with his parents."

It reminds me of the time Scott was scouting players in a gym in Belgrade, Yugoslavia. As he walked around the gym, a toothless old janitor seemed to recognize his Serbian ethnicity. Scott nodded politely to the janitor, who promptly offered him a shot of a potent alcoholic drink from a rather dirty-looking bottle. Feeling it would be culturally insensitive not to accept this gracious offer, Scott took a drink. Then he continued to walk around the gym, watching the players. Once again he encountered the janitor, and once again the bottle was extended. And once again Scott accepted. This happened a third time, before Scott realized his ability to judge basketball skills was now considerably impaired. He left the gym early.

Building an International Network

Scott's work in the international arena began in 1985, almost by accident. A friend in the pharmaceutical business mentioned he knew some Europeans whose sons were hoping for scholarships to play basketball in the U.S. Back then, the game didn't enjoy the international popularity it does today. Indeed, it was almost unheard of to recruit European players to play in the States. Nonetheless, Scott followed up with his friend's contacts and thus laid the groundwork for a sophisticated network of future international "informants." Since then, his network has expanded to include contacts in Canada, Estonia, Israel, Portugal and Yugoslavia. As an assistant coach at the University of Alabama-Birmingham in 1996-99, Scott recruited three players from Yugoslavia. One of them was Predrag Savovic who subsequently transferred to UH and became one of our finest players.

The life of a globetrotting basketball recruiter isn't all fun and games. Coach Rigot is the first to admit that he has little time for sightseeing on his many trips abroad. Most of his hours are devoted to player observation in gymnasiums, talks with athletes he believes can make a contribution to our program, and meetings with their parents and family to discuss the University of Hawai'i. A case in point was his trip to check out Haim Shimonovich, which Scott remembers like this:

"I spent 24 hours on different planes getting to Israel from Hawai'i. Then I spent 48 hours observing Haim as he worked out in a gym. I then talked with him one-to-one about our interest in having him become part of the Rainbow family. I met with his parents to talk about our basketball and academic programs, answering questions about Hawai'i and the university. Then it was off to the airport and another 24 hours of travel time back home. It's a tough pace to maintain, but that's what it takes to get the kind of student-athletes who will benefit our program — and give them the chance for a quality education at the same time."

Seeking Four-Year Players

Scott Rigot's effectiveness in recruiting international players is matched by his reputation for getting key junior college players. This is partly due to the outstanding job he did in the six seasons he was head coach at Spartanburg Methodist College in South Carolina, from 1990-96. During that period, he coached Spartanburg to a 158-35 record, a remarkable .818 winning percentage. This record is even more impressive when you consider that he inherited a team that went 6-and-22 the year before he became head coach. In his first year in that role, the team had a 20-10 record. Scott was named Coach of the Year on four occasions during his career at Spartanburg Methodist.

Coach Rigot's experiences there helped him establish a broad network in junior college basketball around the country. When he got to UH, however, he recognized that Jackson Wheeler was already the junior college recruiting expert on our team. So to complement Jackson's work, Scott made it a point to pursue four-year players instead of two-year junior college transfers. To do this, he turned to his contacts in Canada and Europe, and it wasn't long before UH men's basketball became the most culturally-diverse college basketball program in the U.S.

I appreciate the disciplined, enthusiastic and professional way that Scott carries himself when he travels to distant places. International recruiting requires an ambassador with special skills. The recruiter must develop a network of foreign contacts that can help identify the most appropriate student-athletes for a Division I basketball team. Then, he must be able to build a sense of trust with both the athlete and his family. Humor, honesty, respect and sensitivity for cultural differences are all essential skills for the successful international recruiter.

Scott has used these strategies to bring a number of fine student-athletes to our team. Unfortunately, not everyone has been as happy about this as we are.

Dealing with the Criticism

Our efforts to recruit foreign student-athletes have come under close scrutiny — and under fire. Our critics say we should do more to recruit local talent and players from around the country. Such criticism has been fueled by NCAA concerns over the recruitment of foreign student-athletes in U.S. college programs. In the spring of 2001, the NCAA sent letters to approximately 60 Division I university basketball programs. These letters requested that the schools investigate possible rules violations regarding foreign players. The NCAA specifically wanted to know if any players had:

- Been financially compensated for playing on any basketball team while they lived in another country — a clear violation of NCAA rules that relate to the professional status of players
- Played for any team with other players who were financially compensated for playing with that team. This would also be a violation of an NCAA rule which stipulates that no Division I college basketball player can participate on what is considered to be a professional team. This would include playing on a team on which other players were compensated financially, even if the recruited athlete himself was never paid for playing. A player in violation of this rule could be suspended from his current U.S. college team for a specified number of games to be determined by the NCAA.

Which is exactly what happened to our six-foot-ten freshman center from Israel. Although he had never been paid for playing basketball, Haim had been a member of an Israeli team that did include paid players. According to the NCAA, this was a rules infraction. Consequently, he was suspended for the first 22 games of the 2000-01 season — the number of games he played for what the NCAA said was a "professional team" in Israel.

While our critics say it isn't worth the time and energy we spend to confirm that our foreign recruits have not violated NCAA rules, I am the first person to support the work Scott Rigot has done to bring these excellent recruits to our program. Why?

First, our business is winning basketball games and I welcome any individual who can make a positive contribution to our team — so long as he is eligible to play — regardless of his home of origin.

Second, the players we have recruited from Canada and Europe have come to Hawai'i for all the right reasons. They are not only superb athletes who want to play basketball, they are also conscientious students who attend classes and want to graduate from a major university. Their goals are to become productive citizens and enjoy a better life.

Third, we live in a global community. It is important for all of us to think about how globalization impacts us. We must avoid responding with any ethnocentric biases or xenophobia. All of us must accept the responsibility of working with people from different cultural and racial backgrounds to make our world a better place.

Idealistic? Impossible? I don't think so. To my mind the Olympic Games exemplify the great sense of connection and respect that develops when people from around the world share similar aspirations. I truly enjoy the international cordiality demonstrated at the opening and closing ceremonies of the Olympics. As we move inexorably toward becoming a truly global community, I believe the efforts of men like Scott Rigot will one day be universally recognized for their positive contribution.

I'm always willing to tolerate criticisms of our international recruiting programs because I believe we are doing the right thing. When you stop to think about it, unless you're a Native American Indian or a Native Hawaiian, all of us are "foreigners" in the sense that we have descended from just about every different culture in the world. To truly meet the challenge of living in a culturally-diverse 21st-Century society, we must be willing to open our minds and hearts to new experiences. What better place to demonstrate a commitment for international acceptance than at the University of Hawai'i, the home of the Rainbows?

Maybe a veteran *Honolulu Advertiser* sportswriter said it best in a column that appeared on July 10, 2001. Here's what Ferd Lewis wrote:

"...part of the spice of Rainbow athletics over the years is that the teams have been everything their nickname had implied. Theirs is a tapestry that comes from here, there, and everywhere. It is having players from Hilo to Haifa represent UH and having fans embrace them regardless of origin.

"Remember the Hawaiian and Israeli flags that used to wave side by side in the Stan Sheriff Center when Yuval Katz performed? Or the fans who held up "Que Beleza!" (That's Beautiful!) signs when Wahine volleyball player Veronica Lima, who is from Brazil, stuffed a shot? People whose views on distant corners of the world are too often shaped by stereotypes or 10-second CNN sound bites also have an opportunity to mix in and get to learn about people that they might not otherwise meet.

"It is part of the universe to which the concept of a university makes reference and a portion UH should retain."

Achieving Excellence in Groups

Scott Rigot's style of teaching, coaching and recruiting provides good examples of how one person can use various components of the Rainbow Circle of Excellence to help a group be successful. The visual teaching techniques he uses to teach new plays and nuances about the game help stimulate fresh mental images that foster excellence.

All groups and organizations need to have a clear collective vision of their goals. Using the visual learning techniques employed by Scott may also be a helpful strategy within your own group to stimulate a potential for greatness. If you are part of a group that is not realizing that potential, it may be useful to have members of your team participate in the visioning process. (See Excellence Activity, Chapter Two.) This can help individuals expand their thinking about the organization's potential and energize the group by giving members a clearer sense of their own roles.

At least two other components of the Rainbow Circle of Excellence contribute to Scott's success. They are passion and enthusiasm for the game of basketball. While that may seem obvious, I've seen his passion to win rub off on players who've been down for one reason or another during the course of a season. I was especially pleased that he kept his enthusiastic glow throughout the 2001 WAC Tournament; it noticeably helped the team maintain a high level of energy and confidence.

Creating passion in a group is always a challenge. But without these attributes, I do not think it is possible to achieve greatness. That's why I'm careful to look for the enthusiasm that applicants exhibit when I interview them for coaching jobs, or when I visit potential recruits. I've also found it helpful to have professionals who are trained in the use of team-building strategies come and share their expertise with our team. It never fails to stimulate a greater sense of excitement among players who may be down, who've lost sight of the role they must play to help us achieve group excellence.

EXCELLENCE ACTIVITY

Building RESPECTFUL Connections In Culturally-Diverse Groups

Our two sport counseling and development specialists take a very interesting approach to cultural diversity. Instead of just thinking about how people may differ according to their cultural, racial and ethnic backgrounds, they encourage our student-athletes to think in much broader terms about human diversity by using what they call their RESPECTFUL counseling model.

This model is comprised of ten factors that commonly influence our lives and distinguish us from others. The list contains some of the specific questions that Dr. Daniels and Dr. D'Andrea use to help build respectful connections within culturally-diverse teams, groups, classes and organizational settings. Members of each group are asked to get to know each other better by introducing themselves using these questions as guidelines.

R Religious/spiritual identity and background (What is your religious background and how has it influenced who you are today?)

E Ethnic/racial background (What do you value most about your ethnic/racial background?)

S Sexual identity (What do you value most about being a man/woman?)

P Psychological maturity (What would you say are some of your strongest points in terms of being a psychologically mature individual?)

E Economic class background (How has your economic class back ground impacted the person you are today?)

C Chronological challenges (What challenges do feel you face as a young man/woman?)

T Trauma and Threats to one's well-being (What traumatic events have you experienced in your life and how have they impacted you?)

F Family history (How has your family affected the type of person you are today?)

U Unique physical abilities or characteristics (What unique physical abilities do you possess and how do they affect how you feel about yourself?)

L Location of residence and language preference (What languages do you speak? Did you grow up in a rural, suburban or urban area and how do you think your place of residence impacted your life?)

When the individuals in a group follow this outline in introducing themselves, they inevitably learn many new and interesting things about one another. Watching the docs conduct this activity in classes that included several of our players, I was very impressed with the thoughtful way each student responded to the questions and by the genuine sense of respect the students showed for the unique cultural differences that distinguished them from one another.

This activity is an excellent tool to use when it's important to build positive and respectful connections among persons from different groups and backgrounds. I encourage you to use this activity if you're looking to help the members of your group get to know each other better. You can modify the questions to best fit the backgrounds and interests of the group. ●

PART THREE

THE POWER IN PEOPLE

Learn from yesterday,

Live for today,

Dream for tomorrow.

— *Bianchi Rossi*

CHAPTER SEVEN

THE EXTENDED RAINBOW FAMILY

Most of the groups I've belonged to have enriched my life. Without question the 2000-01 Rainbow Warrior basketball team was one of them. Other special groups have included my family, the UH coaching staff and various teams I've coached over the years. During my college years, there was my local Methodist Church, led by a charismatic minister who influenced my life and helped shape my values.

Many things make these groups work. First, the people in them are special. They often challenge me to think about myself in new ways, which in turn helps me develop the kind of skills I need to lead an effective, satisfying life. The cultural diversity of the UH basketball team, for instance, challenges me to see the world in new ways. It makes me stretch my thinking about coaching techniques I might use with players whose development has been impacted by dramatically different life experiences.

Understanding and coaching players like Jeep Hilton, Savo Savovic, Haim Shimonovich and Carl English — guys from inner-city New York, war-torn Yugoslavia, the Israeli army and rural Canada — have made me respectful of our differences and proud of the similarities that bind us together. In all these ways, the team has made me more human as a coach and as a person.

The special groups I've belonged to have also helped me feel a valued part of a whole, someone who played an important role in helping all the members achieve collective goals and dreams. Though there were many times during the 2000-01 season when the players didn't like the way I pushed them in practice — or took them out of games to talk about ways they could improve — they continued to look to me for guidance. Morever, they acknowledged the helpful role I played in their development as athletes, students and well-rounded people. Often, after players leave the university, I find out how much they appreciate what the coaching staff did for them. I routinely get calls from A.C. Carter (with us from 1996-98), Marquette Alexander (1998-2000), Michael Robinson (1996-99) and others who want to tell us how much they benefited from our basketball program. They frequently admit to wishing they'd been more open then to learning more about themselves.

Other players are able to express their appreciation while they're still with us. There were many times when Troy Ostler would glance at me during a game because he was discouraged by his inability to make moves that would let him slip by a defender. Sensing his frustration, I would pull him out of the game and offer advice. When he went back in, he was better able to beat his man to the basket, or play more aggressive defense, or grab a rebound. Whenever that happened, Troy would run by the bench and throw me a big smile. It told me how much he valued my advice. Such smiles of validation are some of the special moments that coaches experience.

When I bet the team they could cut my hair off if any of them earned a perfect 4.0 grade point average, and when Lane O'Connor did just that, I felt I had clearly communicated the value our program places on academics. This lighthearted session also helped build a tighter sense of family spirit, even if it meant giving up what hair I had left in the process.

At the end of his college playing career, Nerijus Puida extended his thanks for the opportunity to play basketball and get an education. That is one of the most gratifying things that can happen to a coach. This simple statement of appreciation makes all the time and hard work of coaching worthwhile.

Building Generative Communities

Being part of a group is like holding the keys to a special community. It's an opportunity to learn and grow, and to have our contributions recognized and valued. Some experts in organizational psychology refer to these groups as "generative communities." The term refers to the positive and powerful energy generated by any group — a family, team or organization, for instance — when its members come together to create a stimulating, caring and challenging environment that nurtures excellence. Most successful college basketball teams I have known reflect these characteristics. They included players and coaches who:

- Were respectful of one another
- Genuinely cared about other members of the team
- Were stimulating to be around
- Challenged each other to realize a greater level of their athletic potential

As a result of my coaching experiences, I can clearly see how the components of the Rainbow Circle of Excellence foster the development of growth-producing, transformative, generative communities. To develop these special groups it is essential for individuals to recognize the importance of:

- Promoting a genuine sense of interdependence with one another

- Having a common vision of success
- Demonstrating passion and enthusiasm as they build a positive family spirit
- Communicating effectively with each other
- Providing the support that helps members of the group endure tough times
- Challenging each other to have the discipline to develop new knowledge and skills

You may think that sounds like an ideal — and unattainable — community. And you'd be partly right: ideal groups and communities rarely happen. The fact is, we all live, work and learn in imperfect communities. Yet, despite these imperfections, I have found that we can realize unexpected levels of excellence when we commit ourselves to doing certain things as active members of our community — be it our family, sports team, school, company, neighborhood, union, political party or whatever. Taking an active membership role means being willing to work together, sacrifice together, challenge one another, and support one another to achieve a common vision of success. The 2000-01 UH Rainbow Warriors team wasn't a perfect group by any means, but it was certainly special in the way its members generated hope, inspiration, a sense of collective responsibility and the will to achieve greatness.

The Players Behind the Scenes

One other very important element contributed to the success of our team: our extended Rainbow family. One of the goals I set for myself is to keep nurturing the kind of generative community that the experts write about. Naturally, the coaching staff alone can't do everything that must be done to create such a group. So I depend on other people to help create the kind of community that encourages our players to achieve excellence on and off the court.

Fortunately, there are many people willing to play key roles, from the front office to the back of the house. But they work so quietly behind the scenes that most of our fans don't know who they are or what they do. For that reason I wanted to dedicate this chapter to them. As you learn more about these special people, I hope you'll consider some of the practical things you can do to become a more constructive member of your own group.

I want to thank all of the people who are included in this chapter for being loyal supporters of our teams through good times and bad. Most important, I want to thank them for helping us create the type of generative community and family spirit that lets us maintain our collective vision. Whether or not you're specifically mentioned here, please know that I am sincerely indebted to you for your assistance and loyalty.

Joan Wallace

While my wife is certainly the most important person in my immediate family, she also holds a special place in the Rainbow Warrior extended family. I've been married to Joan — a native of Monroe, Louisiana — since 1963, and she has played the starring role in raising our two adopted and now grown children, Kim and Rob. During our marriage she has not only supported me in my coaching career but has done much to build family spirit in all of our teams. She has made so many behind-the-scenes contributions to our generative community that it's hard to know where to begin.

Joan provides the motherly support that many players find comforting when they get homesick or have a bad game. Typically, she waits down the hall from the Sheriff Center locker room to greet each player with a hug, a kiss and a positive comment about some aspect of their game. Joan also helps ensure that players don't "over-worry" about some weak part of their game.

Before our $5.6-million Nagatani Academic Center was built in 1999 as a part of the UH athletic complex, Joan used her skills as a professional educator to tutor players with scholastic difficulties. It was no surprise that our guys enjoyed working with her; she is an outstanding teacher who has worked with students in Hawai'i's public schools since 1987. Joan's holiday dinners for players, coaches and other members of our extended family are rightfully famous. She not only does an excellent job of nourishing the players' bodies, she also provides social nourishment — for instance, by playing the piano as everyone sings carols at Christmas. (She even tries to keep everybody on key, though this is almost always a losing battle.)

Of course, it's difficult for a generative community to generate energy and positive connections unless its members' bodies and spirits are nourished. By making time to eat, talk, sing and laugh together, we help build growth-producing groups. We celebrate the unique values and goals that bond us, as we strive to learn new ways to lead effective, satisfying lives. If you feel that your group is stuck in an unproductive state of malaise, it might be a good time to think about planning some activity that can generate new and positive energy.

Joan couldn't possibly prepare our holiday events by herself. She has help from several other members of our extended family. Among them: Bob's wife, Domelynne Nash; Lynn Scaduto, the wife of our administrative assistant, Len Scaduto; Barbara Ann Gaty, a loyal, hardworking member of our team's

Booster Club; several student-assistants and, of course, Bobbie Omoto, the secretary for the UH Rainbow Warrior Basketball team.

Bobbie Omoto

Bobbie is a big reason why we've developed such strong family spirit in our basketball program. Her contributions go far beyond secretarial duties and helping prepare holiday meals for the team. Because her desk is positioned in the middle of our office lobby, Bobbie is the first person our players greet when they stop by. She gets to know each individual as she interacts with them on an almost daily basis during the season. She provides information that helps them fulfill their academic responsibilities, offers comforting words of support, and reminds them when their next study hall is scheduled. As a mother figure, she lets our players know they can depend on her to provide help and encouragement during difficult times. She also has a tough side, so she knows how to effectively set limits when necessary. She also reminds our guys that she depends on them to represent the University of Hawai'i at the highest levels of academics and athletics.

To achieve excellence, every group should have a Bobbie Omoto. Although she works quietly behind the scenes, she shows great loyalty to the group, provides support to everyone on the team and promotes a genuine sense of interdependence in her day-to-day dealings with others, helping build and sustain our generative community.

It's important for us to identify and encourage the "Bobbies" in any of our groups. You can never underestimate the important role that these people play, or how they help motivate others in the group to do their best.

Chuck and Barbara Ann Gaty

Giving people an extra boost to do better is a basic concept that's often overlooked by group leaders. Most groups can greatly benefit from the help offered by outside supporters.

Like other successful college basketball programs in the U.S., we have a special way of getting our boost — the Booster Club. Among other things, this wonderful organization holds fundraisers to generate money for our program and helps build positive connections between coaches and players and members of the local community. It also provides the emotional support that student-athletes often need to deal successfully with college life.

Much of this is made possible through the hard work and loyalty of club president Chuck Gaty and his wife, Barbara Ann. Chuck, a retired Air Force offi-

cer who took the reins in 1997, organizes fundraisers, helps coordinate a season's-end banquet with club member Ken Takeuye, manages the club's finances,
and uses his excellent contacts to advise me on community relations. Barbara
Ann is Chuck's constant companion, a good friend to our program, and another
important mother figure who supports our players when they need it most.

In the world of modern college athletics, booster clubs play important
roles in creating resources and offering emotional support. I am genuinely grateful for the time, energy and support that our Booster Club members offer our
team. Of course, you don't need a formal Booster Club for your school, business,
or organization to get this kind of boost. In our quest to lead effective and satisfying lives, we all encounter challenges and stress, and when this happens it's
helpful to have outside supporters to depend on, whether it be friends, family, a
spiritual advisor or a professional counselor.

Physician and Trainer

When one of our players is injured, the first person to his side is usually
either Jayson Goo, the team's athletic trainer, or Dr. Andrew Nichols, our team
physician. These individuals have played critical roles in building our generative
community. They diagnose specific injuries, outline necessary medical interven-
tion, and provide follow-up rehabilitation services to help players return to full
form — confident and motivated to perform once again at their maximum
ability.

Andy Nichols has been a full-time physician at the University of Hawai'i
since 1994. He is also an associate professor at the John A. Burns School of
Medicine at UH. His involvement in institutional athletics goes back to his own
student days. As a four-year letterman swimmer at Stanford University, he com-
peted in the 1976 Olympic Trials. Andy served as team physician for the U.S.
National and Olympic Soccer teams from 1990-92, then practiced family and
sports medicine in California before moving to Honolulu.

Jayson Goo has worked in the field of athletic training for more than 20
years. At the University of Hawai'i since 1985, he has helped more than 4,000
student-athletes. Jayson has been primarily responsible for our Rainbow
Warriors basketball team since 1988.

These two medical pros have accomplished wonders for our players.
When Troy Ostler severely sprained his ankle just before the Rainbow Classic in
December 2000, I was certain he'd be lost to the team for an extended period.
But Andy and Jayson helped him return much sooner than anyone expected.
Jayson even worked with Troy on Christmas Day, massaging his ankle and using

Kineso tape to improve circulation and reduce swelling. After only five days of intensive rehabilitation, Troy was actually able to play a few minutes in the final game of the Rainbow Classic against the University of Tennessee. We lost that one, 69-58, but Troy helped us stay dead even with the nationally-ranked Volunteers until midway through the second half. And it was a real credit to our medical personnel that he was able to play at all.

Besides providing treatments, our trainers and medical personnel offer players a complete range of holistic and personalized services, more than they are likely to receive at most other universities. When a player is injured Andy and Jayson collaborate on an initial diagnosis. They gauge the impact the injury will have on the athlete, then follow up to determine what treatment is best for the player. Their in-depth follow-up techniques measure whether the injury is serious enough to take the player out of practice or games, and whether he is psychologically resistant to push himself to play through the pain. To evaluate the latter point requires an ability to "read" a player, to help him overcome the fear he might further injure himself by playing, and to help him regain his sense of confidence.

When a player is injured, there's no way we'd risk exacerbating that injury by making him practice or play. Still, I've been very impressed with how these medical professionals use various psychological, confidence-building and motivational techniques to help injured players regain their mental and physical strength prior to tip-off. Equally impressive is their ability to see the connections between an individual's body, mind and spirit. Here are a couple of examples of their work during the 2000-01 championship season.

Many of our fans will remember that we had to depend on freshman Phil Martin as our starting forward for most of the season. This was an unexpected development. Normally I like to give our freshmen game experience, but I don't like to have to rely on them in high-pressure starting situations. But Phil's featured role developed because of Haim Shimonovich's 22-game suspension and Bosko Radovic's broken leg. And though he had only limited Division I playing experience, Phil played admirably throughout the season. The young Canadian had one of the best field goal shooting percentages in the WAC — 63 percent — and was named to the 2001 WAC All-Newcomer Team.

An easily-excited individual, Phil suffered frequently from a nervous stomach before games. As you can imagine, that's a common ailment among freshman starters. To help Phil adjust to games, Jayson put him on a liquid diet on game days and shared different strategies for relaxation that would help alleviate the pre-game jitters. As the season progressed I could see how these techniques helped balance Phil's body, mind and spirit.

Knowing how the body-mind-spirit connection affects a person's ability to achieve athletic excellence, Jayson has used other techniques with our players in the training room. Carl English would come to Jayson to have his ankles taped prior to a game, then talk about how nervous he felt. While a certain level of anxiety before a game is healthy, too much of it can affect an athlete's ability to perform at high levels. There were times when Carl's nervousness exceeded the optimum level. Jayson used various techniques for both Carl and Phil to help them gain a sense of "relaxed focusing" prior to game time. I'm convinced that such balancing of Carl's body-mind-spirit before the WAC Tournament games helped him score a career-high 25 points and some crucial baskets in our big victory over Tulsa.

The use of these techniques by our medical personnel helped our players develop new skills to strengthen their bodies. It also empowered them psychologically by helping them gain mental and emotional control. The positive relationships that our trainer and physician built with our players helped to further our family spirit and the generative community in which excellence thrives.

The Academic Support Staff

Given the glitter of the games and the celebrity status bestowed upon star players, it's easy for a student-athlete to develop a bit of a narrow focus. All too often this can lead a player to forget that he is both an athlete and a student. The goals of receiving a good education and graduating become clouded, sometimes even ignored. Certainly we want to achieve athletic excellence as a basketball program. But we are aware that our players are, first of all, students. We are committed to an atmosphere that motivates our guys to realize the highest possible level of academic achievement. That's why our academic support staff is such a big part of our extended family.

Creating and maintaining a vision of excellence that extends beyond basketball is one of our most important responsibilities as coaches. As members of the university community, our vision must include the graduation of every student-athlete at the University of Hawai'i. Many of our basketball players have graduated, but not all of them. We are always working to improve in this area. When one of our players leaves the University without a degree, I take personal responsibility for not having done more to motivate him personally to finish his education.

Today, I'm confident we are on the right road. We have excellent people supporting us as we move to graduate a higher ratio of student-athletes from UH. First, there is Leon Schumaker, the Director of Student Affairs. Leon established the first academic program for UH athletes in 1979 — the Academic Assistance Program. Since then he has helped thousands of student-athletes excel in the classroom and find success after graduation. Leon does many things that help them maintain a hopeful and realistic vision about their education and college degree. This includes, but is not limited to, helping our student-athletes deal with concerns about tuition, housing, books, scholarships, employment and financial aid.

I've watched Leon follow Phil Martin into the academic adviser's office to make sure he was registering for courses that would fulfill his scholastic requirements. I've heard him calling players at the start of a new semester to make sure they complete the proper paperwork to get into student housing. "You need a home to do your homework!" he tells them. Leon's presence in our program inspires and motivates many student-athletes to maintain a broad vision of excellence long after they leave the University.

Another key member of our academic support staff is Adam Lockwood, our main academic adviser since 1994. Adam's primary responsibilities include class scheduling and compliance with university and NCAA regulations. He relates well to student-athletes, having been a college athlete himself. At UH he was a four-year letterman in volleyball, earning All-American honors as a senior. Adam graduated from the University of Hawai'i with a degree in history.

I consider Jennifer Matsuda to be an indispensable academic advisor because, as acting department chairperson, she is in charge of the entire academic assistance program for our athletes. I depend greatly on Jenny, who is extremely knowledgeable about the procedural rules and policies our players must follow to complete their graduation requirements.

She is especially valuable when she helps our players find solutions to their academic problems. Once I met with her and Mike McIntyre to discuss a concern he was having with one of his courses. With no solution in sight, Mike was becoming more and more depressed about the situation. But Jenny refused to let him be victimized by his own frustration, and she immediately began brainstorming strategies he might use to handle the situation. This not only helped Mike solve his problem, it made him feel much better about his ability to do so in the future.

I really respect Jenny for her never-say-die approach to helping our players stay on track. Jenny also supervises the other academic advisers — Sara Nunes-Atabaki, Denise Tsukada, Amy Bair and Hyun Underwood — the people who monitor tutoring services, for instance, or contact a professor if a player is doing poorly in a class. Together these advisers provide the structure and follow-up that many of our players need to realize their potential for academic success.

Dr. Ron Cambra, Associate Dean for Academic Affairs, has been invaluable in maintaining our academic support programs. Ron insists that our players are students first and athletes second. Also, while he maintains high expectations of our players, I have seen him give them every chance they need to graduate from our university. This combination of high expectations and support goes a long way toward helping them succeed. Ron is much more than an associate dean; he is a friend and genuine advocate of our student-athletes. Thanks to his commitment and leadership, our academic support programs are the best they have ever been.

The Winthrop Berry Scholarship Program

One critical area of support, of course, is the financial kind. In our business, that means scholarships. In University of Hawai'i men's basketball, Caroline Berry is the name to remember in this area. Not only is she a supporter of many community projects, she is also a good family friend. I had many conversations with Caroline over the years about my responsibility to help our players work hard in the classroom and graduate. She told me she and her late husband shared similar values. Then she set to work founding the Winthrop Berry Scholarship Program in his honor.

To demonstrate the Berrys' commitment to our team members beyond their playing days, Caroline proposed a matching-funds scholarship program. She raised and pledged $300,000 to this new program, provided the Booster Club and other interested community supporters could come up with an additional $600,000. With will and hard work, her vision resulted in the creation of a million-dollar scholarship fund for athletes at UH. This generous gift will enable many future players to come to Hawai'i, receive their degrees, then go on to lead effective and satisfying lives.

Enthusiasm and Passion

Generative communities need the enthusiasm and passion that various individuals bring to the group. We are fortunate to have people like that in our Rainbow Warrior extended family. Here are just a few of them.

My friend and loyal Rainbow supporter Ken Takeuye shows his enthusiasm for our team by providing many hours of volunteer assistance in a variety of roles. From helping organize our annual golf tournament to planning our post-season banquet, Ken is always there to lend a hand.

Edith Tanida is our ticket manager, and part of her job is distributing tickets to our players and coaches — tickets that can be given to friends and family members. Edith is like a mother hen when she talks to the guys about rules they must follow when they give away tickets. She sometimes travels long distances with us on road trips, and our players look up to her with respect and admiration.

Dr. Al Saake, another passionate and enthusiastic supporter, spent more than 46 years at UH before retiring in 1990. He held a number of positions during that time, including head coach of men's basketball for nine seasons in the '50s and early '60s. In fact, he is known on campus as "the Father of Modern UH Basketball." Though Dr. Saake is well into his 80s, he still attends games and practices when his health permits.

Derek Inouchi is the Assistant Director of Media Relations. Thanks to his effective communications with the media and fans, our public enjoys some real insights into the workings of our basketball team.

Our hard-working Athletics Director, Hugh Yoshida, holds a special place in our extended family. A tireless champion of athletic excellence, his advocacy of the student side of student-athletes has greatly helped advance our commitment to academic development. Hugh was one of the key people who made the decision to merge the Athletics Academic Office into the College of Arts and Sciences in 1999. "The merger was a big step for us," he recalls. "Now our student-athletes have the luxury of working directly with the academic community, whose mission is to provide them with the best educational experience possible."

Whenever I have a logistical problem at Stan Sheriff Center, I can always turn to Rich Sheriff, Stan's youngest son and now manager of the facility. Another important member of our extended family, Rich works quietly and effectively to make sure that everything is in place by the time the first fans file into the arena on game nights.

Three other members of our basketball family work long, hard hours behind the scenes. These are our team managers — Matt Brummel, Brian McMullen and Mike McDivett. These guys issue our equipment, maintain the locker room, set up the court for practice (water, towels, balls and so on), pack and handle our gear for road trips and even do the laundry on the road. Although their jobs are far from glamorous, they always fulfill their responsibilities with enthusiasm. This can generate a much-needed boost when the players or coaches are running low on their own supply of energy.

Our fantastic cheerleaders, the talented Rainbow Dancers, and the UH Band never fail to energize our fans. Anyone who has ever seen them perform knows exactly what I mean when I say they are the most enthusiastic supporters of all. Their passion is genuinely uplifting.

Promoting Responsibility and Discipline

To build good family spirit, community members must also be responsible and disciplined. A fine teacher of these key values is Art Woolaway, a familiar face on our team since 1968. As a volunteer administrative assistant, Art handles assignments on the bench and serves as my personal consultant. A genuine teacher, he constantly takes time before and after our practices to talk to players about the history of Hawai'i, the lessons he learned as a standout athlete in four different high school and college sports, and the importance of being a responsible and contributing member of one's community. In many ways, Art is the voice of reason, wisdom and responsibility on our team.

Another valued member of our family is Len Scaduto, an administrative assistant since 1964. Len's primary job is assisting me with community relations and other off-court affairs. During our games and practices, he also tracks player statistics on shots, rebounds, assists and turnovers. His other duties are varied and sundry, including helping me and restaurateur Don Murphy raise funds for the Coaches vs. Cancer program, a fundraiser for the American Cancer Society.

When our players spend time with Len, they learn about his long and distinguished coaching career at Oaklawn High School in Illinois, where his basketball team won 411 games in 29 seasons. He was inducted into the Illinois Coaching Hall of Fame in 1990 and the Northern Illinois University Hall of Fame in 1991. Len also spent three seasons as an assistant coach at Chaminade University in Honolulu.

Len contributes a great deal to our team simply by encouraging discipline and patience. I can picture him walking up to Savo after that difficult loss to the sixth-ranked Tennessee Volunteers. Savo was still steaming. Len, eight inches shorter than Savo, looked into his eyes and said, "If you don't stay focused and disciplined, and follow the game plan, we won't win many games."

A Sense of Community Responsibility

Remember the metaphor of the tree? That it's not so much "the bark we wear" but "the fruit we bear" that really counts? As highly visible members of the community, coaches and players can do a great deal to promote the public good. Our vision of excellence definitely includes social responsibility, and we always try to stimulate awareness among our players about the importance of giving back to the community. At Christmas, for instance, we frequently load our vans and travel to a local hospital to visit with children who are sick. All of us benefit from these visits. The young patients are pleased and excited that their favorite players took time to make a personal visit. The players are humbled by the challenges faced by these youngsters and their tenacity in dealing with seri-ous illness.

I also enjoy working with individuals who want to make a difference in the lives of the less fortunate. That's why I agreed to be a part of the American Cancer Society's Coaches vs. Cancer project. I've worked closely in this effort with the affable Don Murphy, owner of Murphy's Bar & Grill in downtown Honolulu and another important member of our extended family. Don is the kind of person who works behind the scenes to help build our generative com-munity. For instance, Murphy's is also the venue of "Call the Coach," a weekly radio program featuring coaches and players from a variety of UH sports.

As an enthusiastic supporter of UH athletics and a devoted member of our Booster Club, Don has worked tirelessly for Coaches vs. Cancer. We make public appearances together, promoting the cause on radio and television, and challenging our friends and associates to match our monetary contributions. Partly as a result, the UH men's basketball team has been recognized as the nation's second largest contributor to the program — behind Syracuse University. The fact that I received the American Cancer Society's National Coach of the Year award in 2001 was largely due to Don Murphy's commitment to work with me in this worthy cause. I always hope that our efforts in this area encourage our players to be positive, responsible contributors to their communi-ties — far beyond the world of college basketball.

The "family" members in this chapter are just a few of the people who help the Rainbow Warrior basketball program achieve excellence. Their unique contributions help create the foundation for us to grow and prosper as a true community.

EXCELLENCE ACTIVITY

Helping to Build a Generative Community

The 2000-01 team was able to do many things during the season toward becoming a "generative community." One of the ways to build such a commu-nity is the willingness of individual members to do things that have a positive impact on the group, team or organization. Dr. Daniels and Dr. D'Andrea fre-quently use their Pulse Activity (see Chapter 3) with our players, coaches and support personnel to help develop the kind of positive connections necessary to create a generative community within our team. We typically did this activity immediately following our practices and found it to be particularly beneficial when we took our team's "pulse" on game day.

There are other strategies you can use to help build a special sense of community within your own group. Take a few minutes to think about some of the specific things that would help your family, group, team, school or organization more closely resemble a generative community. What might generate more positive, respectful and productive connections among individuals? Think about what you can do as one individual to help create a more positive family spirit. Then promise to do two practical things that might help promote a generative community in the days and weeks ahead. ●

Many people make up the Rainbow Warrior extended family. That includes
our high-energy UH band (*top*) and the basketball program's long-time secretary and
"mother figure," Bobbie Omoto, shown here on Senior Night with Coach Jackson Wheeler,
Coach Bob Nash and Todd Fields.

We've got extended family — like these young fans (*opposite, top*) awaiting a Troy Ostler autograph — and immediate family, too (*opposite, bottom*): my daughter, Kim, her husband, Chad, and my grandson, Jackson Riley Haynes.

More "family" members: UH cheerleaders (*above*) and students with plenty of school spirit.

Top: Singing carols at the Wallace household is a Christmas tradition.
In fall 2000 I said I'd shave my head if any player earned a 4.0 GPA. When Lane O'Connor got
straight A's, the guys took turns with the clippers at the Christmas party (*above*).

The last home game of the season is Senior Night, when players leaving the team are honored with leis and accolades. The 2000-01 seniors (*top, left to right*) were Nerijus Puida, Todd Fields, Lane O'Connor and Troy Ostler. *Above*, Haim Shimonovich and I chat with our play-by-play radio announcer, Bobby Curran, during the "Call the Coach" radio program at Murphy's Bar & Grill.

Lane O'Connor lets one fly in a mid-season match-up with TCU.

CHAPTER EIGHT

THE DOCS:
PERFORMANCE ENHANCEMENT
AND LEADERSHIP TRAINING

In 1997-98 we had a terrific team. Most of our fans probably remember that season's Rainbow Warriors, led by Anthony "A.C." Carter and Alika Smith. A.C. and Alika were an unlikely combination — the gutsy point guard from Atlanta and his sharp-shooting, homegrown counterpart from the island of O'ahu. The media called them the "dynamic duo," and for good reason. They helped us beat nationally-ranked Indiana, 82-65, in the season opener and two weeks later led the team to a stunning upset of then-number-two ranked Kansas, 76-65. For a couple of weeks in the middle of that season the Rainbows were ranked number 23 in the country.

But shortly after that national ranking, we went into a slump. We lost to a couple of teams I thought we should have beaten. We were out of sync, not playing up to our potential as a cohesive unit. Something was missing from the team chemistry. I knew we needed something, but I wasn't sure what.

Meanwhile, two professors in the University's Department of Counselor Education, both avid basketball fans, were as frustrated as we were. On the morning of January 27, 1998, I received a letter from them outlining their experience as performance enhancement consultants and sport counselors. After I'd read their letter and reviewed their resumes, I called and invited them to my office.

If you knew what a control freak I am, you'd appreciate what a big step it was for me to meet with a couple of sport counselors. I'm very protective about what goes on with our team and, frankly, I'm not wild about outsiders butting in. But because we were genuinely searching for ways to reverse the slump, I swallowed my pride and made the call.

Getting to Know the Docs

As we shook hands that morning, Dr. Judy Daniels struck me as friendly, serious and well-educated. I wasn't sure what to make of Dr. Michael D'Andrea. He looked kind of like Jesus with his shoulder-length hair and full beard. But first impressions aside, it didn't take long for me to realize that these two were very knowledgeable about the field of sport counseling. They already possessed keen insights into the psychological makeup of the team and individual players. Early in our meeting I pointed to the roster on the wall and asked them to go down the list for me, assessing the strengths and weaknesses of each player.

They handed me a two-page proposal entitled "Promoting the Optimal Performance of the 1997-98 University of Hawai'i Men's Basketball Team." Well, I thought, at least they're organized. I soon discovered they were more than just organized. In their proposal they had listed the team's strengths and weaknesses from a sport psychology perspective. They had also outlined some of the specific performance enhancement services they thought they could provide to help the players regain their focus.

I had to admit their assessment dovetailed nicely with my own. Here's how they listed our strengths:

- The 1997-98 UH men's basketball team is special.
- It has already demonstrated its potential for greatness by beating number-18 Indiana and number-two Kansas.
- It is a team that effectively uses a complex offensive plan devised by its coaches.
- The players have shown that they can be disciplined and focused in executing this plan.
- The players have shown that they can effectively implement the defensive strategies that the coaches have set for them.
- This team has a special chemistry that is marked by the players' unselfishness and their willingness to play through injuries.
- The players have shown that they have a lot of heart and soul in playing the game of basketball.
- This team has captured the respect and admiration of everyone in the state of Hawai'i.

In outlining the team's weaknesses, the professors pointed out that:

- Despite the talent and heart the team has shown, there has been a great deal of inconsistency in player performance over the last few games.
- They have lost two of their last three games.
- The team's three-point shooting percentage is down.
- The team's overall foul shooting percentage is down.
- The number of unforced turnovers is up, which might reflect a loss of concentration and focus among some of the players.
- While the defense is still strong, there are occasional lapses in players' ability to focus, which has led to too many easy baskets for opponents.

- Overall, there has been a change in the level of concentration and focus, which seems lower than it was earlier in the season. Not only can this lead to a lessening of the overall performance, it can cause some players to become frustrated and down on themselves, the coaches and other members of the team.

In their proposal Drs. D'Andrea and Daniels also listed specific performance enhancement and sport counseling and development services they believed could help:

- Setting up individual interviews with coaches and players to get their impressions of the team's strength and weaknesses
- Providing individual and group goal-setting services
- Leading team and individual visualization exercises
- Conducting individual relaxation, focusing and biofeedback exercises for players

I was impressed by these strategies to help our guys realize higher levels of athletic excellence. But beyond their professional competence and manner of presentation, what I really liked about "the docs" — as we came to call them — was their genuine and positive manner. At that first meeting they were careful to caution me against any quick fixes. "We don't want to give you the impression that we can perform any miracles," they told me. "But we do believe these techniques can help get your players' heads back into the game. By letting them focus on their strengths, listening to their concerns and frustrations, and offering them these various performance enhancement services, we think we can help you and the other coaches."

It sure sounded convincing. And it seemed that Michael and Judy wanted to work with us for all the right reasons. I also sensed that this might be the kind of fresh breeze our team needed at that point in the season. We could bring a new sense of positive thinking to student-athletes who were beginning to let their frustrations and self-doubts interfere with their playing ability. So based on these first impressions, I did what many who know me thought could never happen: I gave a couple of "shrinks" a chance to work with our team.

Group and Individual Performance Enhancement Services

From that day on, the docs were invited to almost all of our practices. They observed the way our players and coaches were interacting. They evaluated the level of energy and focus of each player. They assessed how the team was working together as a group.

Then they interviewed each of our coaches and players individually. These meetings were used to get to know the guys as individuals and to explain the various performance enhancement techniques. At first, some of the players really didn't want to work with the docs. "I don't need to talk to any 'sport counselor' about my game," growled Mike Robinson, one of our key players. "Don't need to and won't!"

"Look, Mike," I said, "maybe they have something to offer you and the team that can help us somehow. Why not at least give them a chance? Just talk to them a little." As it turned out, Mike met with Dr. D'Andrea on many a Saturday to get tutoring help in some of his tougher courses. He also became one of the docs' strongest supporters.

The docs were correct about one thing: they didn't perform any miracles for us during the 1997-98 season. But during the seven weeks they worked with that team, they definitely had a positive impact on the players' performance. In hard numbers alone, here's how they summed it up in their report to me at the end of the season:

- A slight improvement in team field goal shooting percentage, from 43 percent before their arrival to 45 percent afterward
- A slight improvement in team free throw percentage, from 67 to 70 percent
- A noticeable decline in average turnovers per game, from 16 down to 13

While these figures were by no means earth-shaking, they were improvements nonetheless. I was aware that the docs had only worked with the team for about seven weeks and the way I saw it, any upturn was welcome. But more important to me than the statistical improvement was the way we seemed to get back on track psychologically. I could see where the docs' involvement with the team was helping us form the kind of generative community I was seeking.

The players had begun to warm up to the performance enhancement activities. More often than not, they discovered that some of the techniques and services helped them perform more effectively on the court. The more popular services that helped our guys included — in the language of sport counselors and psychologists — visualization, guided imagery and relaxation training; meditation; teaching ritualized and anchoring athletic strategies; team-building activities; goal-setting training; and leadership training. As the docs continued their work, the players seemed to give them greater respect. I soon began to notice that the docs' regular presence at practices was having a positive influence on both players and coaches. I frequently kidded the docs about being "the most positive people I've ever met," but I really wasn't joking. Their sense of optimism and hopefulness was as contagious as it was genuine.

After reviewing the evaluation report at the close of the 1997-98 season, I decided to extend our arrangement. Today I can see what a good decision this was, for it has given me a chance to learn new things about sports psychology and performance enhancement — and about my players too. The lessons have been beneficial for our teams and the two professors have become important members of our extended Rainbow Warrior family.

As they continued to work with us, the docs also learned plenty about the ups and downs of college basketball. With their help, we shook off the slump and finished the 1997-98 season with a 21-9 record, falling just one win short of getting to the final four of the National Invitational Tournament. With the departure of A.C. and Alika, we struggled to a 6-20 record during the 1998-99 season, but rebounded in 1999-2000 to 17-12. Then came the magical 2000-01 season of trying times and splendid rewards, including the WAC Championship and a trip to the NCAA Tournament. Through these ups and downs, the docs continued to work with us. They built close relationships with the players and coaches and they expanded their performance enhancement services. In the process, they made us all aware of what it means to take a "holistic approach" to sports counseling.

The Holistic Approach

Before the 1999-2000 season, the docs met with me during the summer to talk about their interest in taking what they called a more "holistic" approach with our team. They would do this, they said, by emphasizing various services designed to enhance players' academic, career and personal development as well as promote their athletic performance. Dr. Daniels described research that shows how participation in sports positively affects college students' psychological development and sense of well-being. She stressed four areas that any successful coach knows are important for athletes to master if they're going to be successful at the college level:

- Effective communication skills
- Goal-setting skills
- Learning to effectively manage one's emotions in times of stress
- Acquiring the inner power necessary to overcome the roadblocks that interfere with one's ability to achieve life goals

As I listened to Dr. Daniels, I had to laugh at myself. All these years, I'd been emphasizing the importance of these very skills to my players. Yet I had mostly been stressing their importance in athletic competition. What I was learning from the docs was that I'd been teaching life skills all along. I just needed to help players see how these skills could be used in all aspects of their lives. Then Dr. D'Andrea asked me what I told my players just before a big game. Well, I said, I routinely:

- Reminded them of the need to communicate with one another during the game
- Urged them to keep focused on the game plan that I had set up for them, reminding each player of specific plays they'd need to use to attain our goal of winning
- Emphasized the need to remain calm and disciplined during the game
- Explained that while I had faith in their ability to meet any challenge they would face in the game, they would also have to make the individual and collective efforts necessary to overcome the hurdles presented by the opposing team

Of course, the similarity between this list and Dr. Daniels' life skills list wasn't lost on me. Though I was well aware that college basketball provided young people unique opportunities to learn about life, the docs were stretching my thinking about new ways our program could help promote players' total development. This included using the basketball court as a special kind of classroom in which my coaches and I could do different things to foster players' athletic, intellectual, moral, social and academic potential. In doing so, the docs said, we'd be taking the kind of holistic approach that encouraged student-athletes to ready themselves for life by realizing their own unique leadership potential. Then Dr. Daniels told me about a new course she'd be teaching that fall, one that offered a perfect way to further enhance this leadership potential.

Learning Leadership in the Classroom

The course was called "Human and Organizational Leadership Development: Theory and Practice." It was open to any registered undergraduate student at UH and was co-taught with Dr. D'Andrea. To my knowledge, it's one of the first undergraduate courses open to any student that integrates leadership theories with sports psychology. In class, the docs teach their students how to use various performance enhancement strategies that sport counselors and psychologists commonly utilize in their work to achieve excellence in their own lives. These strategies include visualization, guided imagery, meditation, goal-setting and other self-improvement steps to realize their leadership potential.

Many of the students who take this class are student-athletes from a variety of teams: football, men's and women's basketball, baseball, softball, women's soccer and Rainbow Wahine volleyball. Dr. Daniels tailored the material to help students link the class with the unique challenges they face as college athletes.

In her new course Dr. Daniels asked her students to ponder the impact of America's cultural diversification on groups and organizations. She showed them how school and business leaders often fail to meet the challenge of cultural diversity. She talked about promoting more positive and respectful connections in group settings. While I found her lectures interesting, I wanted to know specifically what the course would do to help our players deal with challenges in game situations. So I sat in on several of the classes to preview the material and see how our students were responding.

To begin, Dr. Daniels told the class she wanted to learn more about their individual backgrounds. She hoped to gain a better understanding of how their unique cultural experiences influenced their development. An effective leader, she explained, must understand how such experiences influence the way members of the group think and act.

She passed out a worksheet listing specific issues she wanted the students to address as they introduced themselves to the class: where they grew up, the number of brothers and sisters they had, two people who had influenced their character development, and so on. As I listened from the back of the room, I heard heartfelt stories from the students about how their cultural and family backgrounds had affected their lives. One player kept the class spellbound as he recounted the fear he felt growing up in a war-torn country in eastern Europe. Another tried to explain his mixed feelings about the high rate of alcohol abuse he saw in his beautiful but underdeveloped community in rural Europe. Another student spoke with pride and conviction about his service in the armed forces, and the constant threat of violence that surrounded him. Another shared the strength he had gained from the anger and insecurity he felt when his mother abandoned him.

After each person introduced himself or herself, the others asked thoughtful questions. Now I could better understand how Dr. Daniels was helping the students gain an appreciation of cultural diversity, while building respect and a deeper understanding for each other.

In the classes that followed, she employed a broad range of performance enhancement techniques. First she would demonstrate them, then encourage the students to practice the techniques in the classroom under her supervision. They included:

- Relaxation and guided imagery techniques to more effectively manage stress

- Visualization exercises to help seek higher levels of success in different endeavors
- Biofeedback to control emotions and feelings
- Positive self-talk strategies to build confidence in specific tasks
- Goal setting to pinpoint specific improvements in life
- A self-improvement plan requiring the description of specific academic and personal goals.

What I saw in her class further convinced me that the docs could benefit our athletic program in many ways. And, of course, this view was reinforced by the help they gave our team at the end of the 2000-01 season.

Helping Us Win on the Road

Our team has never been very successful on the road. Our record over the past 30 years shows what a tough time we have outside Hawai'i. I've even wondered if some kind of a curse follows us whenever we leave the friendly confines of Stan Sheriff Center. For most of the 2000-01 season, this "road curse" continued. Our away-game record was a frustrating 0-7 — 0-12 if you went back to the previous season. In late February 2001, we were facing our last road trip of the season, one which would include the WAC championship tournament. In the WAC it works this way: whatever a team's record during the regular season, anyone who makes it into the tournament still has a chance there to win the conference championship. It was a critical point in the season for us; we had just won three important home games, but our overall record was a modest 13-12. And that wasn't the kind of record that would be given much consideration by the NCAA or NIT tournament selection committees. How could we break the road curse?

My coaches and I had tried a number of different things during the season to help us win on the road. We changed practice times at our destinations. We used different motivating talks before our games. Our players always seemed to practice hard on the road. They appeared confident that they could win, despite the discouraging record.

As we prepared to leave on that final trip, the docs appeared in my office. "You might not like these ideas," they said, "but before you throw us out, we want you to consider some suggestions we have about winning on the road."

In their search for solutions, they had interviewed all the coaches, trainers and managers. The docs had combined their recommendations along with some of their own to come up with the following list.

- Make sure the players don't sleep on the plane ride to the West Coast. (Our first game of the trip would be at San Jose State University.)

Keeping them awake during the flight, then letting them sleep in San Jose, would help them maintain a normal schedule. From a leadership perspective, co-captains Troy Ostler and Nerijus Puida should be delegated to periodically patrol the aisles to keep the guys awake and focused on the team's mission.

- Have each player keep two bottles of water on the plane and drink from them often to avoid dehydration.
- Ask the players to keep their TV sets off late at night so as not to disrupt their sleep patterns and to protect their Vitamin A and D reserves.
- Have the entire squad, including coaches, lie down in a circle at center court after each practice — eyes closed, backs to the enemy's floor — and visualize the excitement of playing back in Stan Sheriff Center.
- Schedule nightly meetings to let the players talk about what each of them would commit to our victory. These meetings would also provide a forum for the guys to voice any concerns or disagreements they had with other team members. The docs could then walk the players through these concerns toward a positive resolution

All of these suggestions sounded reasonable to me. I endorsed their plan and felt more optimistic about our chances of ending the curse. Before we left, the docs explain the new road strategy at a team meeting. None of the players objected; they were just as tired of losing on the road as I was and were willing to try anything to succeed.

The result? We broke the curse in the first game, beating San Jose State 71-61. We ruined the Spartans' Senior Night and moved up into a three-way tie for fourth place in the standings. Savo posted a game-high 29 points, including three 3-pointers. Carl English came off the bench and scored 13 points in the second half alone.

At the end of this game we all gathered in the locker room. We were ecstatic and full of energy. I called the docs into the locker room to celebrate with us and said to everyone, "The docs came to me with a plan. I agreed to use that plan on this road trip. You all bought into it and that's how we broke the road curse. We are a family. We are going to continue to be a family and work hard to show everyone what we are capable of achieving before this season is over. And as we continue together I want all of you to remember this saying: 'You have got to believe!'" The players hooted, hollered and cheered wildly — partly for the docs and partly in celebration of what it's like to achieve excellence over the rainbow.

Unfortunately, the docs had to return to Honolulu the next day to teach. We continued on to the University of Texas at El Paso. It was the final game of the regular season, and despite playing what I thought was our best road game of the year, we lost to the Miners, 85-77. It was time to call the docs. I knew we needed them to help us win the WAC tournament. We had built a family, but it was incomplete without the docs and their daughter there. I asked them to meet us at the WAC Tournament, which would start the following week in Tulsa. I wanted them around to maintain the positive energy and family spirit we had created as a group.

The rest is Rainbow Warrior basketball history. We went on to win three of the toughest road games of the year — against TCU (99-79), Fresno State (76-67) and finally homecourt favorite Tulsa (78-71). We had learned how to win on the road.

Helping to Build a Family Spirit and Sense of Community

While all the docs' suggestions played a part in our success, I believe those nightly team meetings were a key component. They helped build positive family spirit and strengthened the sense of group connection and interdependence we needed to play up to our potential. Building this special sense of community may have been the docs' greatest contribution. In all the seasons since they started with us in 1996-97, they have rarely missed a practice. Dr. Daniels worked with the players even when she was pregnant, and starting just a couple of days after Mahealani was born, both mother and daughter made sure to show up at practice.

Judy is a reliable resource on academic and personal issues. Michael has an ever-optimistic spirit that is highly contagious. Obviously, I'm thankful that these two UH faculty members took the time to write that letter to me, and that they agreed to share their knowledge of sports psychology and performance enhancement skills. Their consistent interest, loyalty and support for our team has had a lot to do with the way our players and coaches have accepted them into our extended family. Recognizing the positive contributions they have made to our team, I decided to make them an even more integral part of our family by taking them along on all of our road games, starting with the 2001-02 season.

EXCELLENCE ACTIVITY

Completing Your Own Self-Improvement Plan

One of the assignments that Dr. Daniels gives students in her Leadership Course is to complete a Self-Improvement Plan. Reflecting the holistic philosophy that she uses in her work, this plan is an excellent tool for helping students focus on specific things they need to do to realize their potential for excellence.

I include it here as an Excellence Activity because I believe it can help anyone chart specific directions toward leading a more effective, satisfying life.

SELF IMPROVEMENT PLAN

I. Personal Improvement
1. List two personal strengths that you possess (e.g., "I am thoughtful/honest/outgoing.")
2. List two personal weaknesses (e.g., "I procrastinate. I get nervous when I'm around lots of people I don't know.")
3. List two things you'll do in the next month to improve yourself in these areas. It is important to be as specific as possible here.
4. Briefly state how you'll know that you've actually improved in these areas. Be as specific as possible.

II. Academic/Career Improvement
1. List two academic (or career) strengths that you possess (e.g., "I am hard-working and conscientious.")
2. List two of your academic (or career) weaknesses (e.g., "I do not participate in class discussions. I get extremely nervous when I have to take an exam.")
3. List two things you'll do in the next month to improve yourself in these areas, being as specific as possible.
4. Briefly state how you'll know you've improved in these areas. Again, be specific.

III. Athletic/Physical Improvement
1. List two of your athletic strengths (e.g., "I'm a good defensive player. I'm in good condition.")
2. List two of your athletic weaknesses (e.g., "I'm not shooting very well from the foul line. I'm out of shape.")
3. List two things you'll do in the next month to improve yourself in these areas.
4. Briefly state how you'll know you've improved. ●

CHAPTER NINE

SEASONS IN COACHING

Our coaches are effective because, more than anything, they help our players develop new ways of thinking. Basically, we use the basketball court as our classroom. Throughout the season I watched Bob Nash at practices, huddling with Troy Ostler, Todd Fields, Haim Shimonovich, Phil Martin and Mindaugas Burneika — giving them new ideas about playing the "big man's game" in the front court. I saw Jackson Wheeler working with Savo Savovic, Lane O'Connor, Nerijus Puida and Ryne Holliday, teaching them new moves they could use to play smarter, more effective defense. And I can still see Scott Rigot in a flurry of animation — waving his arms as he explained the finer points of the guard position to Mike McIntyre, Jeep Hilton and Lance Takaki.

Coaches teach many issues unrelated to basketball. One of the wonderful things about being a college coach is the way we can use the athletic arena to cover the fundamentals of basketball as well the importance of becoming life-long learners.

Life, of course, is our greatest teacher. As a coach, I try to connect frequently with my players, to keep in touch with what's going on in their lives. This lets me learn new things about each individual, and to help him think in new ways about his personal and academic responsibilities.

Bob Nash often comes to practice early to talk with players. I remember his heart-to-heart with Haim Shimonovich on the bench about how the Israeli was adjusting to this new country. I overheard the practical suggestions Bob offered Haim about coping with change, and his advice to use his experiences to learn new and positive things about himself. Jackson Wheeler always has players in his office before practice, guys who come in to discuss personal or academic issues. Much more than just a coach, Jackson is a personal adviser. Scott Rigot starts the counseling process even before his international recruits leave home — helping them visualize what it's like to live far away on a tropical island. He describes the "aloha spirit" and how many people find it the most appealing aspect of living in this unique place. Scott helps our student-athletes think in more expansive ways about the world beyond their borders.

Effective teachers use different communication techniques to stimulate thoughts and images about the world. Of course, you don't have to be a great orator to be an effective teacher. But it helps to communicate with other people in ways that help them see things from a different perspective. The true test of a great teacher and coach is the ability to communicate a hopeful vision of the future, and to motivate others to realize their individual and collective vision of greatness.

Many of the effective teachers and coaches in my life had the ability to tell interesting, enjoyable and inspirational stories. These stories had common characteristics. Often they were about the rewards to be had for those willing to invest in hard work, discipline and cooperation with others.

Why do people enjoy listening to a good storyteller? Some stories stimulate new and positive images of the world. Others arouse pleasant feelings in the listener. Many stories offer different ways of thinking about life and inspire people to make changes.

One of the greatest communicators of the 20th Century — a wonderful storyteller — was Dr. Martin Luther King. A powerful teacher and a passionate orator, he helped people see the possibilities in their future. He inspired millions to make difficult sacrifices as they worked together to realize a common vision of racial equality.

In different ways, the popularity of John F. Kennedy, Ronald Reagan and Bill Clinton was directly linked to their ability to communicate effectively with motivational stories. Each of these men was able to help people see things from a new perspective. They also made folks feel good about being Americans, and they inspired our decision makers to implement policies favorable to their administrations. Whether you liked these men or not, you have to acknowledge that much of their success was related to their communications skills. They inspired people to work toward new goals for our nation.

Because storytelling is a such an effective way to inspire people to greatness, we use it whenever possible in our coaching. At the conclusion of practice on game day, coaches and players meet at center court, where they clap their hands in unison for a couple of minutes. This is a mental ritual that helps us focus on the challenge of the upcoming game. When the clapping stops, I tell a short story. The stories typically focus on a previous encounter we've had with the team we're about to play. Of course, not all of these "stories" have plots or dramatic endings. Sometimes they deal with the things our players need to do to win the game, like keeping their focus, staying disciplined or responding to different defensive strategies. Sometimes they describe the unique qualities we possess as a team, like being more "together" than our opponent, or using our family spirit to overcome long odds.

After our practices at the 2001 WAC Tournament, I told the players the same story before every game. I began by reminding them that anything can happen in a tournament. Then I told them about the 1993-94 Rainbow Warriors, a team that entered the WAC Tournament with a mediocre 15-14 record, then played inspired basketball to beat archrival Brigham Young University for the championship and earn a trip to the Big Dance. Our players seemed to enjoy the similarities, as well as the picture I was trying to paint for them.

Using Metaphors to Promote Excellence

Over the years I've learned that metaphors can be very useful in helping people develop new images of themselves. Technically speaking, a metaphor is a figure of speech in which a word or phrase ordinarily meaning one thing is used to designate another, to make a comparison.

Basketball coaches, players, fans and sportswriters are famous for using metaphors. A player is described as being "ice cold" when he's lost his scoring touch; another with tremendous jumping ability is a "sky walker;" a player or coach is called for a technical foul because he "crossed the line" with a referee.

Metaphors are also used to describe unique athletic characteristics. "Air" Jordan refers to Michael Jordan's uncanny ability to fly through the air on his way to the hoop. "Twin towers" refers to two very tall players who play on the same team — most notably, David Robinson and Tim Duncan of the San Antonio Spurs. Many people still remember the phrase, "The doctor has made a house call," referring to the way Julius Erving — "Doctor J" — would "operate" on Philadelphia 76er opponents back in the '70s and '80s.

Earlier I described our team as a "sailing ship" with myself as the "rudder" and Bob Nash as the "anchor." And I characterized Coach Wheeler as a "mountain of endurance" for his ability to remain positive in the face of great adversity. By using these metaphors, I hoped to create distinct, memorable images of the strengths these individuals bring to our team.

Following are a few metaphors from nature, to help illustrate the various tasks and challenges we face as coaches throughout the year. Growing up in rural Illinois, I spent a lot of time outdoors — playing and working, hiking and hunting and learning the nuances of the changing seasons. Today, I see my work year as a sequence of four "seasons," each one characterized by its own unique challenges.

Springtime: Planting Seeds for Success

The first cycle of my coaching year starts in mid-August, when our student-athletes return to campus to resume their studies. I refer to this as our "planting season." A successful harvest, of course, begins with a good job of planting seeds. From June to September I meet with my coaches and do just that: we lay out our vision for the season ahead and discuss strategies for realizing the greatest level of team success.

Later in the planting season, I talk with all of the players. I want them to get a clear picture of what we aim to accomplish athletically and scholastically. This is the time when the coaching staff shares a collective vision of group goals. It's also the time when we outline what each individual needs to do if we're going to realize that vision.

The spring season also includes the beginning of formal practices. This is when the players are challenged to learn new plays and condition themselves for the work ahead. By NCAA rules, our practices can't officially begin until mid-October. At the University of Hawai'i, we formally celebrate the opening of practice season with what we call the Midnight 'Ohana — 'ohana being Hawaiian for family.

At our Midnight 'Ohana, all the players and coaches on the men's and women's basketball teams are introduced to our fans. Then, just after midnight, when practice season is officially open, we conduct a few shooting and dunking drills and stage an intra-squad scrimmage.

What I like about the term "Midnight 'Ohana" is the way it affirms the idea that we're all part of a large family — coaches, players, support personnel, fans. From the beginning of the season, we try to instill the value of working beyond individual interests — promoting teamwork, cooperation and positive family spirit.

This family image, of course, is often used by schools, businesses and community groups to encourage interdependence and personal connection. Even if your group hasn't yet used the family metaphor, there will surely be many opportunities for you to do so in the future. The start of each new academic year is an excellent time to introduce this image in the classroom. And if your business is changing personnel, for good reasons or bad, the family image can offer positive reassurance in the workplace.

Summer: Warming to the Task

Summer is the time of year when things really heat up. It can also be a period of growth and development. In the world of college basketball, the "summer season" is the onset of the team's regular conference schedule. Our players are challenged to demonstrate their growth and development while our coaches work hard to prevent any "weeds" that might crop up and result in a less than successful harvest.

Our "weeds" are a tendency of some members of the group to break away from the team concept. Some players start to lose sight of our collective vision. They might be players who are frustrated because of injury or lack of playing time. They might be student-athletes who are failing or doing poorly in certain classes. To prevent these weeds from growing and undermining a successful season, coaches, trainers and other support personnel are challenged to do several things. Coaches can continue to build the team's sense of unity, to prevent individual players from fragmenting into subgroups, focusing on individual interests or losing sight of collective goals. Trainers can alleviate the frustrations of injured players, helping them recover physically and psychologically. Counselors and office staff can support team members with academic or personal problems.

Fall: A Good Harvest?

The fall season is harvest time. For basketball coaches and players, harvest time occurs during conference tournaments, when everything a team has learned during the regular season can really pay off. A successful harvest requires an unusually high level of discipline and enthusiasm, to consistently and effectively execute game plans under intense pressure. Everyone must demonstrate a willingness to accept and carry out their delegated roles. They must be prepared to respond to the unexpected challenges that occur during tournament play, such as injuries or travel delays. Harvest time requires all members of the team to work together to realize its collective vision of success. The rewards for a college basketball team during harvest season are definitely worth a year of hard work: a conference championship, a berth in the National Invitational Tournament or a trip to the Big Dance — the NCAA Championship Tournament.

Naturally, group members are more likely to achieve excellence if they have a clear image of the rewards. Teachers do this when they lay out clear goals at the beginning of each course. Companies schedule staff retreats to give employees the chance to share their hopes and concerns in a relaxed setting. The Rainbow Warriors do this with short, post-practice meetings on game days. These sessions help the players stay focused by emphasizing their individual and collective strengths. And they remind them that the game ahead is yet another step on the road to achieving our goal.

Winter: A Time of Reflection and Celebration

The final part of my year is winter, which for basketball coaches extends from late March through late May. It's a time to reflect on the events during the rest of the year, to celebrate the harvest, and to acknowledge the contributions and sacrifices of others. In the world of college basketball, this is the time when coaches are working to sign new recruits as they plan for the next spring season.

Effective leaders recognize the importance of taking time for reflection and celebration. These leadership strategies serve different but complementary purposes. Time for reflection lets individuals regroup, rejuvenate, center themselves, and analyze the ups and downs of the past year. Celebration time can be used to reinforce the unique roles of each individual, their accomplishments and sacrifices, in the pursuit of group goals. Our annual banquet at the end of each season always acknowledges individual and team accomplishments.

Using Seasons in Other Group Situations

Using the images of the four seasons might help you think differently about your own team, group or organization. For instance, you might apply the images of the four seasons to changes in your family. The birth of a baby or a marriage might symbolize the beginning of a new spring when seeds of hopefulness are planted. Or you might recall when a family member started school or got a new job, beginning a kind of summer season of growth, discipline and renewed enthusiasm.

A family's harvest time might be marked by someone's graduation from school or promotion at work. That's always an occasion for celebration. Even retirement or the death of a family member aren't viewed as negative events if we see them as a necessary part of the winter season. Rather, these natural occurrences provide a unique time to reflect on the meaning of what's important in life, and to foster more meaningful connections.

Similar metaphors from nature can be used in companies and other groups. Too many people say they've fallen into a rut with their spouses, or at work, or in their social lives. And while thinking in metaphors won't eliminate your frustrations, it can be very helpful in creating new and positive images. The main idea is to think outside of the conceptual boxes that may be limiting your ability to lead a more effective life.

Treating Players Appropriately, Not Equally

Many people are limited by their customary ways of thinking and acting. These days, you hear a lot of talk about "thinking outside the box." Here's an example of how we do this with the team.

If I said, "Coaches should treat their players equally," most people would undoubtedly agree. The truth is, this statement is an excellent example of thinking within the box. It also reflects a rather shortsighted view of human diversity. I would argue that it's more respectful and effective to treat players "appropriately" by acknowledging and responding to their unique strengths and weaknesses.

For instance, even when two of our players are the same age and come from the same socioeconomic, cultural or racial backgrounds, they commonly think and act differently from each other. On the basketball court, I've found that they usually fall into one of three general categories. I call them Creative Street Players, Team-Oriented Players and Reflective-Thinking Players. Individuals in each of these categories have consistent strengths and weaknesses, which a good coach not only understands but uses to help the whole team realize its goals.

Given the unique differences of these three types, it isn't right or effective to use the same coaching techniques with all of them. Of course, every student-athlete needs to follow established team and university rules and policies, as well as the laws of the land. And when a player violates these rules and laws, we impose the same disciplinary action across the board. But when it comes to a player's style and level of psychological development, that's when we use different techniques and strategies to fit the individual.

Creative Street Players

Creative Street Players use their street smarts to outwit opponents. By following their instincts and their impulsive tendencies to take the ball to the hoop, they can catch opponents off guard, then finesse their way into scoring position. There's a downside to such players. They commonly disregard the offensive and defensive strategies of their team as they let impulsive energy control their actions. They also run the risk of frustrating other players who are trying to implement the game plan.

Savo Savovic shows tendencies of being a Creative Street Player. On the plus side, there are times when he plays with an intensity that neutralizes an opponent. This helps energize our team, especially if our game plan doesn't happen to be working at the moment. The obvious problem is that this style of play undermines a more disciplined, patient and team-oriented approach to basketball — which, in the long run, is a more effective way to win consistently.

My coaches and I have worked hard with Savo to help him develop a more team-oriented approach to his game. Our coaching strategies with him are different than with other players. We acknowledge his creativity and skills as a plus when used at the right moment, but we constantly try to make him a more disciplined player. Savo has developed a lot since he joined our program, and his willingness to balance his creativity with a more team-oriented style has made him a more effective member of our team.

Team-Oriented Players

Team-Oriented Players work hard to remain disciplined and implement the game plan. They bring to the team very different strengths and weaknesses than the Creative Street Player. Team-Oriented Players are distinguished by the unselfish way that, for instance, they make the extra pass to a teammate who's in a better position to score. On the downside, a weakness of the Team-Oriented Player is a failure to take an open shot when he has it.

Once an opposing team senses you're a Team-Oriented Player, it can work against you. Your man is more likely to play off you on defense in order to help double-team another player with the ball. Although the Team-Oriented Player may get more assists than his teammates, he will also enable the defense to put more pressure on other players.

This was a problem for Nerijus Puida when he joined the team. He was such an unselfish, team-oriented player that the word got out around the league that he would rather pass then shoot. While we consistently praised him for his leadership, we constantly encouraged him to shoot more. We tried to have Nerijus develop the ability to keep his opponents guessing. We wanted his defenders to constantly wonder: "Will he pass the ball or shoot it? Should I play him tight on defense?" But to make his opponents think like this, Nerijus had to move beyond being the ultimate Team-Oriented Player. As the 2000-01 season progressed, he quickly became a much more well-rounded, less predictable player — and a big reason why our team was able to win key games down the stretch.

Reflective-Thinking Players

This type combines elements of the Creative Street Player and the Team-Oriented Player. When a more creative play is required, even though it might deviate from the game plan, the Reflective-Thinking Player will use his judgment to make the right move. When the situation demands a disciplined, patient approach, he does his best to execute the plays we have repeatedly gone over in practice. On the downside, Reflective-Thinking Players have a tendency to be overly critical of their performances. Often they get caught up in a negative assessment of their play choices.

Mike McIntyre is a good example of a Reflective-Thinking Player. He consistently demonstrates the kind of discipline and patience that is necessary to be an effective Team-Oriented Player. But his flexibility allows him to surprise any defender who takes him for granted, perhaps taking a three-point shot when his defender thinks he's going to pass the ball. But sometimes, Mike gets too much in his head. He'll think about his mistakes and what he might have done in different situations. This causes him unnecessary frustration with himself, his teammates and his coaches. Thus, he has to be coached differently than a Savo or a Nerijus. I ask him to stop thinking so much about mistakes and focus more on his successes. I remind him that making a mistake isn't a sin. What is almost a sin is being so self-critical that you don't realize your own level of excellence.

I'm proud of Mike McIntyre's progress and development during his three years as a Rainbow Warrior. He learned that there are times to turn on his creative side, and he learned when to remain a disciplined, patient, team-oriented player. Now Mike is less critical of himself when things go wrong. Instead of being consumed by negative thoughts, he can channel his energies in a different way. He can remain positive and focus on what he can do even better the next time.

These are just three examples of the different player types you find on a basketball court. Bottom line: there's no way you can coach or treat them all the same way. The same is true in other fields. Many parents, teachers and business managers, for instance, use this approach to treat their kids or students or employees "appropriately" rather than "equally." It's simply a more thoughtful, more effective way of working with people. As leaders we must think outside the customary boxes that limit our ability to realize true potential. Only in this way can we tap the unexpected dimensions of personal power and realize the dreams buried in our hearts and minds.

EXCELLENCE ACTIVITY

Self Talk: Building a Positive Inner Voice

Each of us has an inner voice that sends us messages about how we are performing in different situations. Sport counselors and psychologists refer to these messages as "self talk." Research has confirmed that self talk has a definite impact on the way we perform various life tasks. As you might guess, negative self talk is associated with losing and poor performance, while positive self talk is associated with winning and improved performance.

In several of my meetings with Drs. Daniels and D'Andrea, they talked about the potential power of positive self talk, as well as the adverse effect that negative self talk has on people in general and college athletes in particular. They discussed several training strategies they wanted to use with our players to help them increase and maintain positive self talk and emotional power. These strategies can be very useful in enhancing not only the performance of college athletes, but anyone else interested in achieving a greater level of effectiveness and satisfaction in their lives.

Steps to Positive Self Talk and Emotional Power

Step 1: Be aware of your inner voice and how your self talk impacts your academic, career, athletic or personal performance.

Step 2: Recognize that most of us have an internal critic that uses a negative voice to remind us of our weaknesses. When this voice dominates our self talk, it can overemphasize the negative aspects of our perform ance and downplay our positive potential. To avoid this, try to reframe your negative self talk by thinking about your weaknesses as areas for improvement and developing new strengths.

Step 3: Make a commitment to replace negativity with positive self talk. Sport psychology researchers have shown that optimal performance occurs when individuals are in control of the kind of self talk that goes on inside their heads. Therefore, it is important to train your mind to notice negative thoughts and immediately replace them with positive ones.

Step 4: Focus on the present and hear yourself make suggestions about specific ways you can improve a situation, rather than getting down on yourself for past failures or becoming depressed when you fall short of achieving a short-term goal. Remember, positive self talk involves the constant reminder that you can achieve success with continued effort!

Step 5: Acknowledge your improvement when you successfully achieve a task that you've focused on doing right.

Step 6: Use the list of affirmations provided below or create your own list to maintain positive self talk.

Affirmations

"I will always give 100% effort!"

"Once I set goals for myself I will always strive to reach them."

"I don't like the present situation, but I can cope with it."

"I don't have to be perfect to achieve my goals. I need to focus on my best effort."

"Things didn't go my way, but it's not the end of the world. I look forward to the next time."

"I know how to keep cool under pressure. It's not such a big thing."

"I never stop learning. I can always improve."

"My mistakes give me feedback, showing me where I can become stronger." ●

Chapter Ten

The Right to Dream

I t is a distinct honor for me to serve as head coach of the University of Hawai'i men's basketball team. Since I took the reins in 1987 I've worked to help student-athletes realize their potential for excellence on and off the court. In the process I've been fortunate to work with players, coaches and other members of our extended family, who have taught me about the positive things people do to lead effective, satisfying lives. The Rainbow Circle of Excellence is an overview of many of these things.

I hope the stories in these pages have helped you to better know and appreciate our Rainbow Warrior family. More than that, I hope they've helped explain the concrete steps we take in the pursuit of greatness, to help our team realize its collective vision of excellence.

By now you know that my definition of "greatness" has less to do with fame and fortune than it does with a commitment to self-improvement, and to helping others to do the same. These are the real rewards of the greatness I encourage in my players, because I believe we are all capable of achieving it in our lives.

When we follow the principles of the Rainbow Circle of Excellence, there are three important things to remember:

- We must each understand and realize our own personal power
- We must avoid falling prey to the cynicism of our times
- We must exercise our right and responsibility to dream

Understanding Our Personal Power

Achieving excellence in life requires knowing how personal power can be used to create successful outcomes. While this may seem obvious, I notice how little time people take to really reflect on their own personal power, and the ways it can be used to attain excellence in life.

Why do so many people avoid thinking about their personal power? Tony Robbins, the internationally renowned motivational expert and author of the best-selling book *Unlimited Power*, answers that question this way:

"Power is a very emotional word and that is one of the reasons why people have varied responses to it. For some people, power has a negative connotation. Some people lust after power. Others feel tainted by it, as if it were something venal or suspect...To me, ultimate power is the ability to produce the results you desire most and create value for others in the process. Power is the ability to change your life, to shape your perceptions, to make things work for you and not against you."

Like Robbins, I think of power as the ability to make things work for you, not against you. I'm fortunate to be in a position, as head coach of a major college basketball program, where I can help people discover untapped aspects of their personal power and use them in all aspects of their lives.

We encouraged Savo Savovic to move beyond his creative, street-game playing style to become a more team-oriented player. We reminded Nerijus Puida that he could become a more effective athlete if he tapped into his unrealized ability. That required him to evolve from the ultimate unselfish team player into a more aggressive offensive shot-maker. By demonstrating the will power and discipline to think outside of the box, Nerijus was able to tap into new dimensions of his game.

But if tapping our potential is so easy, then why aren't more of us doing it? Studies show that most people use less than 30 percent of their overall physical abilities and less than 20 percent of their mental powers in the course of their lives. Why? One of the major factors is the way we manage time. Many of us get so caught up in our busy daily lives that we wind up exhausted, spending the evening in front of our television sets. Almost no time is set aside to think about achieving greater levels of personal excellence.

I believe that people find it helpful to hear about how others have realized excellence. When these stories are about people we know, they encourage us to better manage our own lives and discover new dimensions of personal power. It is my hope that the stories about our championship team and our extended family will help you think about using the Rainbow Circle of Excellence to promote the collective power of your family, team, group or organization. I know that learning about the successes of others has worked for me. It has motivated me to devote the time and energy to find my own untapped power as a husband, father, coach and teacher.

Avoiding the Cynicism of Our Times

Your renewed efforts to draw upon your personal power might be met with skepticism. In these cynical times, some people might even criticize your new, more positive attitude — might call you impractical, a dreamer. But don't let pessimists distract you from your goals. My belief that we could win the 2001 WAC Tournament was often met by disbelief. Had I let these negative observations affect our focus and motivation, we might not have pulled it off. Though other teams in the tournament boasted greater talent — one was nationally-ranked — I refused to listen to the cynics who said we didn't have a chance.

When I encounter pessimistic people, I remind myself of the famous Robert Kennedy quote: "Some people see things as they are and say why. I dream things that never were and say why not." One of the best things about being a college coach is the opportunity to work with wide-eyed, positive young people. All of the players on our 2000-01 team carried that sense of hopefulness and boundless optimism throughout the WAC tournament. While it was their hard work and discipline that got us through the tournament undefeated, it was the dream of success in their minds and hearts that let us achieve excellence over the rainbow.

Exercising Our Right to Dream

The ability to create a vision of excellence cannot not be understated. It isn't a special skill available to just a fortunate few. Anyone can do it but — like the other components of the Rainbow Circle of Excellence — it requires a strong commitment to tapping under-utilized human potential.

In the rush of day-to-day living, few of us take the time to exercise our right to dream about a better future. Nor do we spend much time thinking about what we can do to make it happen. As I coach I use my dreams to move our team forward during the season. I submit that it's not only our right but our responsibility to dream.

Everyone would benefit, for instance, if parents took more time to dream about what they want for their children. Teachers have a responsibility to dream in order to more clearly visualize effective ways to teach. Business people have a responsibility to dream about creating a workplace that values each and every employee. Even children have a responsibility to dream of ways to make the world a better place.

When we were in Dayton, Ohio, for the NCAA tournament, we arranged for our players to visit Kennedy Elementary School. The players talked with the kids about basketball and also shared some of their hopes for themselves and their families. It was an inspirational moment when Lance Takaki described how he overcame his short physical stature to become a Division I college basketball player. And it was a happy moment when big Troy Ostler lifted the kids up to a basket in the auditorium so they could dunk the ball. The smiles on those youthful faces reflected a real sense of pride and excitement. They felt larger than life. They were dreaming big dreams.

Anyone who wants to lead a more effective life and realize more personal power must be willing to exercise their right — and responsibility — to dream. It means pushing aside cynical views and taking the time to visualize the possibilities.

The 2000-01 Rainbow Warriors did just that by focusing on the collective vision we shared as a team. They put aside cynicism and pessimism. They kept their eyes on the prize. They worked hard as an interdependent group to realize excellence over the rainbow. I hope their story helps give you a push in the right direction. And I hope you'll think about our championship season as you strive for excellence in your own life.

EXCELLENCE ACTIVITY

Group Questions

This final activity is a simple one that the docs use with our players at the beginning of each season, to help them think about how they might strive for excellence in the months to come. Like the other Excellence Activities in this book, this one can easily be modified to fit the needs of your own group. I think you'll find this simple exercise helpful in clarifying what the members of your group mean by "excellence" — and useful in building the cohesiveness that's so important in realizing a group's real potential.

Ask the members of your group to write brief answers to the following questions. Then have them read their answers aloud. Write the responses on a large piece of paper or poster board on the wall. As the members begin to share their ideas, it is important for the leader to help the members of the team process the various responses.

1. What does the term "excellence" mean to you?
2. What does this team or group need to do to realize its potential for excellence?
3. What are two things you are willing to do to help this team or group achieve excellence?
4. What is one thing you are willing to give up to help this team or group achieve its potential for excellence? ●

CHAMPIONSHIP SEASON 2000-01

Louisville 86, UH 71

United Airlines Tip-Off Tournament
UH 59, Southeastern Louisiana 55
San Diego 65, UH 63
UCLA 84, UH 64
UH 86, Texas-Pan American 73

Hawai''i-Nike Festival
Georgia State 65, UH 64
UH 76, California State-Northridge 70
UH 100, Alabama-Birmingham 86

Outrigger Hotels Rainbow Classic
UH 81, Manhattan 67
UH 75, St. Louis 67
Tennessee 69, UH 58

Western Athletic Conference Season
Texas Christian 103, UH 64
Southern Methodist 69, UH 56
Texas, El Paso 79, UH 71

UH 68, Tulsa 65
UH 65, San Jose State 64
Rice 70, UH 64
Tulsa 79, UH 67
UH 91, Fresno State 73
UH 76, Nevada-Reno 69
Nevada-Reno 73, UH 60
Fresno State 86, UH 63
UH 79, Southern Methodist 65
UH 61, Rice 53
UH 102, Texas Christian 87
UH 71, San Jose State 61
Texas, El Paso 85, UH 77

Western Athletic Conference Tournament
UH 99, Texas Christian 77
UH 76, Fresno State 67
UH 78, Tulsa 71

NCAA Tournament
Syracuse 79, UH 69

2000-01 Rainbow Warriors

Name	Height	Weight	Class	Hometown
Mindaugas Burneika	6-7	225	Jr.	Kaunas, Lithuania
Carl English	6-4	178	Fr.	Patrick's Cove, Newfoundland, Canada
Todd Fields	7-0	252	Sr.	Mesquite, Texas
David Hilton	5-11	145	Fr.	New York, New York
Ryne Holliday	5-10	150	Jr.	Belleville, Illinois
Phil Martin	6-7	198	Fr.	Ontario, Canada
Mike McIntyre	6-3	205	Jr.	Long Beach, California
Lane O'Connor	6-7	211	Sr.	Vancouver, Washington
Troy Ostler	6-10	205	Sr.	West Valley City, Utah
Nerijus Puida	6-5	195	Sr.	Sakiu Raj, Lithuania
Bosko Radovic	6-9	220	Fr.	Montenegro, Yugoslavia
Predrag Savovic	6-6	225	Jr.	Herceg Novi, Yugoslavia
Haim Shimonovich	6-10	245	Fr.	Rishon LeZion, Israel
Lance Takaki	5-4	135	So.	Honolulu, Hawai'i
Ricky Terrell	6-3	190	Jr.	Los Angeles, California

The winningest coach in University of Hawai'i basketball history, Riley Wallace has been the school's head coach since 1987. He was both a player and a coach at Centenary College in Shreveport, Louisiana, where he still ranks among the school's all-time leaders in both scoring and rebounding. The Illinois native also earned a master's degree in education from the University of Illinois. At the University of Hawai'i, Coach Wallace has led his teams to numerous National Invitational Tournament appearances and to the NCAA championship tournament in 1994 and 2001. He was named the Western Athletic Conference's Coach of the Year in 1989 and 1997. Riley Wallace lives in Honolulu with his wife, Joan. The couple has two children, Rob and Kim, and a grandson, Jackson Riley Haynes.

Judy Daniels and Michael D'Andrea received their doctoral degrees in Human Development Counseling at Vanderbilt University in Nashville, Tennessee. Since 1989 they have been professors in the Department of Counselor Education at the University of Hawai'i-Mānoa College of Education. They have worked extensively with adolescents and young adults from a broad range of cultural, ethnic, racial and socioeconomic backgrounds. Drs. Daniels and D'Andrea are nationally recognized leaders in the counseling profession, having published more than 100 journal articles, book chapters and other scholarly works. They have also co-authored three textbooks that are widely used in the fields of counseling and psychology. Their daughter, Mahealani D'Andrea Daniels, born in 1999, is their constant companion and inspiration in life.